TEXTURE OF THE GOSPELS

Four Perspectives, Four Textures, One Powerful Story

☐ ───────── ☐

Simply tell the greatest story ever told.
Experience Jesus Christ first-hand from the Gospel
'closest to where you are.'
Never underestimate the power in that simplicity.

☐ ───────── ☐

2nd Edition

James Utley, PhD

Dedication

Over the years, I have written a lot. Most of it has been used by small groups of Christians seeking to understand God's will for our lives better. In this second edition of this book, I hope to provide a workbook that helps the reader see Jesus more closely.

I have been fortunate to have so many wonderful influences to do this work. Amazing pulpit ministers, including Lonnie Ritchie, Andy Kizer, and the late Darrel Rickard. Outstanding college professors John Fletcher, the late Bailey McBride, and Avon Malone. More importantly, my Dad, Jim Utley, encouraged me to teach and write at every opportunity, and co-teachers like Dan Squires and Paul Arvin made that a pleasure. Daughter Lydia who designed the book cover and loves everyone, and daughter Chloe who likes to wrestle with theological ideas with her brother Josiah and our amazing daughter-in-love Abigail; they all reflect a better me than I am.

Most importantly, my amazing wife, Julie, has been by my side for three decades of preparing Bible studies. She has tolerated countless moments of "let me read this to you and see if it sounds right." If anything in this book sounds right, she is the only reason.

Table of Contents

Abbreviations Commonly Used

KJV   King James Version
ASV   American Standard Version
NASV New American Standard Version
NIV   New International Version
RSV   Revised Standard Version
MLB   Modern Language Bible
Moffat Moffat Translation of the Bible
ESV   English Standard Version
Matt   Gospel According to Matthew
Mark Gospel According to Mark
Luke   Gospel According to Luke
John   Gospel According to John
Acts   Acts of the Apostles
Rom   Romans
1 Cor 1 Corinthians
2 Cor 2 Corinthians
Gal   Galatians
Eph   Ephesians
Phil   Philippians
Col   Colossians
1 Thes 1 Thessalonians
2 Thes 2 Thessalonians
1 Tim 1 Timothy
2 Tim 2 Timothy
Tit   Titus
Phlm Philemon
Heb   Hebrews
Jas   James
1 Pet   1 Peter
2 Pet   2 Peter
1 Jn   1 John
2 Jn   2 John
3 Jn   3 John
Jude   Jude
Rev   Revelation

TEXTURE OF THE GOSPELS

Introduction

My hope for this study is simple. I want to gain a richer
personal understanding of the Gospel accounts: Matthew,
Mark, Luke, and John. Specifically, I'm eager to explore
how the style in which each account is written can
contribute to a deeper understanding. I also want to
discover how God used the personality and firsthand
experiences of each author to shape their writing. Then, I
plan to select a few specific passages and, using the
enriched overall understanding I've gained from earlier
study, seek to understand those passages more clearly.
Finally, I'm excited to share these fresh insights. Through
all this, I want to grow closer to the person of Jesus
Christ and invite you into a warmer relationship with
Jesus, the man, Jesus the Creator, and Jesus the Christ.

Throughout these lessons, we'll journey together through
a simple plan: We'll begin with a few chapters getting to
know the Gospel writers and their writings. Then, I'll
share a reading plan and a simplified harmony of the
Gospels. The heart of our study will be eight chapters
exploring each writer's personality and their unique
Gospel perspective. We'll close with Select Studies—
special topics I'm particularly excited to explore with you
in greater depth.

I've included blank pages after key studies for your personal notes. This book is meant to be your companion—please write in it and make it truly yours.

Ideally, you'll use this with friends or your Bible study group. That's how this guide was born—through years of leading Gospel harmony studies. I've found that a 10-week schedule works beautifully for most church groups. With typical 13-week church studies, you can use one week for introduction, ten weeks for reading and discussion, and two weeks to wrap up together.

You'll notice I use the traditional BC (Before Christ) and AD (*Anno Domini*, Latin for 'in the Days of Our Lord') rather than CE/BCE. Since Jesus Christ is what made our calendar common throughout the world, I've chosen to honor that.

While I reference original language insights using Strong's numbers (like H7676 or G2334), I haven't dove deeply into Greek or Hebrew—I'm not a scholar in those languages. Many online resources can help you explore these references when they appear.

I hope you find this workbook as exciting to use as I've found it to write.

Textures

How do we experience life? Do we watch our own lives, as if someone recorded it on film? Life is not as simple and tidy as what we see on TV. Life exists in three dimensions. It is full of smells and tastes; some pleasant, some unpleasant. Life is hot, cold; soft, hard; dark, and light; bitter, sweet; empty, full; fast, slow; broken, whole; loud, quiet; smooth, rough; heavy, weightless; certain, unknown. The life God gave us to experience reaches us through many senses. He designed it that way. Each of us must have our own confidence in God. (Rom 14:22)

God created each of us to be unique. He puts us on different paths to explore various experiences and to enjoy the beauty of His creation moment by moment, specifically for each individual. Even when we have rare chances to share a moment with someone else, we often do not see it the same way. Each person perceives things differently.

If we are comfortable with this idea, why do we struggle with why God provided us with four accounts of Jesus' life? Why do some in the world read the diverse experiences each of those four Disciples had in the presence of our Lord and see discrepancies and conflicts?

Why do we see disagreement instead of a complementary, composite picture?

Some of us look forward to seeing a sunrise with great anticipation, while others would rather sleep in. Some enjoy a quiet evening alone, while others long for the company of a group. Some can stare at the stars for hours, while others prefer to watch a movie. Not everyone prefers the same things, but we can understand why others enjoy what they do. We do not oppose the value of these differences.

We embrace how these plain contrasts contribute to our individual value and importance. It is the very presence of diversity that makes us unique, yet we can still work toward common goals and share similar desires. Each of us resonates most strongly with experiences that align with our personal preferences. The four Gospel accounts work together in much the same way. Each has its own personality but shares the same shared ambition. God gave us four men, each with life experiences that prepared them differently to tell the greatest story ever told.

Matthew, Mark, Luke, and John each record the details of Jesus' life through the lens of their own experience. Each account is fully accurate but written from different perspectives. Just as Philip started in the scripture where the Ethiopian personally stood (Acts 8:35), each of these four inspired men began their account of the Savior from where they personally stood. I will go into more detail about where each writer was in their life that prepared them as we study each book. For the rest of this chapter, I will simply touch on some basic differences between the men and get a sense of each account of our Christ.

If each Gospel has a distinct perspective and thereby a distinct purpose, we can choose which account to rely on based on our current needs. If someone is new to the Church, where can they learn the basics? If someone denies the historical authenticity of the Gospel account, which one emphasizes that most? If we are struggling to reconcile our faith with our works, do we know who wrote the most on that topic? We can learn these kinds of things.

For example, I agree with most commentaries that Mark was the first to be written. Mark was also the youngest Gospel author at the time he wrote it. He is the only writer we know of who was raised in a Christian home (Acts 12:12). This youth, inexperience, and freedom to be excited lead us to a uniquely written Gospel account. Mark writes as though he has no idea what Jesus will do next, and no idea of why each action is important. This is simply because Mark did not know. He records with excitement and surprise with each act of service he sees the Creator perform. He drafts the story exactly as he saw it unfold—no analysis, no conclusions, just excitement for what he saw. He tells the story of Jesus from a firsthand perspective.

It is for this very reason that Mark is such a wonderful place to start when introducing someone to Christ. We introduce someone new to Christ the same way that Christ introduced Himself to Mark; we tell the greatest story ever told and let them experience it firsthand. Mark begins where most of the world finds itself every day. The world has no knowledge of Jesus. Mark does not explain how Jesus' actions fit into the Old Testament or how history interacts with Him. He simply writes what he could 'see.' Think of Mark as the well-worn t-shirt and the most tattered pair of work pants. He is the ordinary guy we find pleasant in our workplace or helping us fix a flat tire. Mark's gospel has calloused hands and dirty knees. Everything about the feel, taste, and experience of Mark is familiar. Never underestimate the power of that simplicity.

In much the same way that Mark assumes the role of storyteller for Jesus, each of the other writers similarly uses their own experiences to write in complementary styles and for complementary purposes. Luke writes as a historian, making sure that those who come after him can accurately place the life of Jesus accurately into the context of world events. Matthew acts as a teacher, correctly connecting Jesus' actions to the predictions and preparations that came before Him. Finally, John is the theologian who draws on his extensive experience to explain why many things happened and why they must continue to happen.

Luke is the only known Gentile writer in the New Testament. As such, he is familiar with not being accepted. He was also a physician, highly educated, and very aware of his outsider status. He puts significant effort into making sure those on the outside know that Jesus is for them, too (Luke 2:32). Luke records Jesus' longest speeches on the value of individuals (Luke 15) and notes Jesus touching those who love Him (Luke 7:45). He also works hard to ground the account of Christ firmly in verifiable historical evidence (Luke 1:1-4).

It is for these reasons that those familiar with some aspects of the Bible's teachings but who doubt its authenticity or feel alienated by its message can find guidance and comfort in Luke. Luke is the writer who shows how Jesus can help. His Gospel is like a warm coat on a cold day and sturdy hiking boots on rough terrain. It is like the professional-looking stranger who unexpectedly hugs us. Everything about Luke's Gospel, from the kind words to the reassurance of accuracy, is soothing.

□ ─────────── □

Simply tell the greatest story ever told.
Experience it first-hand from the Gospel 'closest to where you are'.
Never underestimate the power in that simplicity.

□ ─────────── □

Matthew was an Apostle to Jesus Christ who left a lucrative career as a tax collector. He is intelligent and calculating. Personal gain clearly motivated him; otherwise, he would not have chosen Roman tax collecting as a Jewish man. However, he encountered overwhelming evidence that Jesus was the Christ foretold in ancient scriptures (Matt 5:17). This awakened his sense of national heritage, spurring him to action, and he recognized Jesus as David's true successor to the throne (Matt 1:1). Matthew carefully explains why and how we can look forward to the future while appreciating our past heritage (Matt 5:43-48).

Those who have become disillusioned or are unconvinced that the entire Bible speaks with integrity about God and His promises will find Matthew compelling. Matthew's excitement about Jesus, who fulfills the purpose of all those who came before Him, is contagious. His Gospel is like a passionate teacher whose enthusiasm is so overwhelming that students cannot help but learn and love their newfound knowledge. Matthew is the pressed pants and neat shirt— the person in the back of the room who suddenly understands what the teacher has been saying all along and lets out a clear 'a-ha.' Everything about Matthew's Gospel is fulfilling and stabilizing.

John is the ironic writer. While he was a simple fisherman by trade (Matt 4:21), John had the benefit of many years of reflection on what everything he saw meant. He was among the most trusted Apostles (Mark 14:33), Jesus' best friend (John 13:23), and caretaker for Mary (John 19:26). He alone of the first followers lived into old age. From that old age, through measured reflection, he presents a Jesus who is absolute deity and creator of the universe, the only source of eternal life, yet a personal friend.

Those seeking to see the face of God and understand His love for humanity will find it here. John's theology is complex and compelling. He is not a polished theology professor; rather, he resembles more of a 'village elder.' He is like an old suit of clothes, worn past its prime, covered in the cares and knowledge gained only through a lifetime of experience.

God motivates and brings together Mark, Luke, Matthew, and John—storyteller, historian, teacher, and theologian—each from contrasting backgrounds for a single purpose. Through their distinct styles, each writer emphasizes different aspects and sensations of the Christ experience. The following pages present an abbreviated table highlighting the basic and unique characteristics of each Gospel.

Yr	Written From	Gospel Accoun	Author	Purpose	Unique Characteristics of each Gospel	Key Verse
50	Rome	Gospel of Mark	Mark, son of Mary	"Jesus the Servant"	Most use of descriptive action of the Gospels; vivid color commentary (Asleep in the 'stern' of the boat 4:37; 'loved' the ruler 10:21; took children up in his arms 9:36, 10:16; 'green' grass 6:39). Of its 661 verses only 31 are not essentially repeated by Matthew or Luke. Most use of Aramaic to quote Christ. Most use of Latin idioms. Word "Law" never used. Word "Immediately" used 41 times.	Mark 10:45.
58	Caesarea or Rome, (Paul in Prison)	Gospel of Luke	Luke, Gentile physician	"Jesus the Savior of the Lost and Rejected"	Only known Gentile author in the New Testament, Luke focuses on the personal relationships Jesus had as well as his interaction with "outsiders". The chronological gospel. More women than other gospels. More sick/crippled than other gospels. More 'outcasts' (tax collectors, prodigals, etc....) than other gospels. More of Jesus' individual prayers than other gospels (Luke 5:16; 6:12; 9:28-29; 11:1-13; 18:1-14; 22:32, 44; 23:46). Greek sentence structure is the "most educated" NT writing. Relationships are called out as very important. Luke 9:51 to 18:35 is unique to this gospel and not found in any other writings. Only account of the Prodigal Son and supporting passages.	Luke 19:9-10

| 58 | Antioch in Syria | Gospel Of Matthew | Matthew, Apostle and Tax-collector | "Jesus the fulfillment of the Law and the Prophets" | Most use of reference to the Old Law of any Gospel; often called "The Bridge Between" the OT and NT. Matthew comes first in all ancient manuscripts of the canon. Calls Jesus the "Son of David" more than all other Gospels combined (1:1; 9:27; 12:23; 15:22; 20:30, 31; 21:9, 15). Written from the perspective of a Jew speaking to Jews; uses 'Rabbinical logic.' Uses the term "fulfill" more than any other Bible book (1:22; 2:15, 17, 23; 4:14; 8:17; 12:17; 13:35; 21:4; 26:56; 27:9). Matthew states that 1) God did something completely new with this Testament, and at the same time 2) we cannot do away with, but rather must embrace, a fulfilled Old Law (5:17, 21, 27, 31, 33, 38, 43). | Matt 5:17 |
| 85 | Ephesus | The Gospel Of John | John, Apostle and fisherman | "Jesus: Lord and Creator" | Miracles and allegories of 'sight' tied to 'water' and 'life'. Strongest exploration of the question "who IS Jesus?" Sometimes called the "reasoning" gospel as it explains not only how to follow Jesus, but WHY we would want to (1:14). John paints a picture of the Jesus whom the disciples saw every day, and their interactions. This is why John focuses on the third year of Jesus' ministry, and why he records some of Jesus' 1-on-1 conversations. One of the most complicated metaphor architectures in all literature. John cites "three sevens", "four images", coming in 'my name', 'signs, witness and testify, obeying 'he who sent me', 'keep my commandments', with time we 'now understand what he said'. (Birth 47x, Water 53x, Light 68x, Sight 168x) | John 20:30-31 |

Gospel Reading Plan

We cannot live the joy the good news of the Gospel brings if we do not know what it says. Starting to read the Gospels can seem daunting. With a plan in place for what to read and when to read it, you can bring the task down to size.

There are many ways to approach reading the Gospels. For this study, I recommend reading all the Gospels in a harmonized fashion, geared toward reading larger sections whose order enhances the reading experience. For this study, we are interested in exploring the diverse experiences presented by each writer, aiming to gain a deeper understanding of each text individually and thereby enhance our comprehension of the whole.

□ ———————— □

Before reading a large section of the Bible,
decide how much you will read over what period of time
and commit to a daily reading plan.

□ ———————— □

I have selected the authors we will read in what order, based on progressing from a simple story to a detailed story and context, and ultimately to lessons learned. In most cases, this means we will read Mark's account first, then Matthew, then Luke, then John; this order typically emphasizes what we could see if we were there, how that ties to what went on before, what we will do with that information, then how we feel about it or how it affects our relationship with God. Sometimes that order is changed to Mark first, then Luke, Matthew, and John; in this order, we will characteristically see the experiential story first, how it fits into current events or social situations in the first century next, why those current events occurred because of past events, and finally how that affects our Theology. The reading orders as selected are my opinion. I chose them based on what order will help our exploration of the Gospels. I am referring to this approach as a "Simplified Harmony" of the Gospels.

I designed this Reading Schedule so that we will read 70 to 100 verses per typical day, for five days each week, which leads us to reading all the Gospel account in 10 weeks. Seventy verses to 100 verses represents about the length of two average-sized chapters, which is a very manageable size. Most average readers will find this takes 10 to 20 minutes. I do recommend reading the entire daily read in a single sitting, not in interrupted parts. I also recommend setting aside a specific time of day each day to do the reading. If you want to do it in the morning, do it every morning. If you prefer noon or evening, be consistent with that. I have designed this plan so that you read 5 days a week, we can study together as a group on one more day, and you do personal study on the remaining day each week. That personal study could be journaling time, a deeper dive, or simply re-reading passages that are calling to you. I included a column that shows how many verses I scheduled for each reading, what reading day of the week I designed each to fall on, as well as a column labeled "Done," making it easy to mark the date you complete each reading.

The following are notes on a few alternative approaches to reading the Gospels. These are common ones I did not select for this Study. Each is good in its own respect but is better suited for other kinds of study.

Canonical Reading: In this approach you read Matthew, Mark, Luke, and John in that order; the same order in which the Canon of scripture organizes them. This is the most common approach. This is a fine approach, but if you want to get a feel for how the books compare with one another, time separates some of the accounts to such an extent that comparison becomes difficult. Additionally, this approach prioritizes the literary style of each book over its purpose. What I mean is this: Matthew's literature is in the style of a Teacher who assumes you already know much of the story and focuses on bringing out notes about how Jesus fulfills the Old Testament.

In contrast, Mark is a storyteller who focuses on what you could see as an eyewitness and makes efforts to transport you mentally to that place and time. Luke takes on the role of detailed historian, recording the most accurate account about order and current events, as well as the names and roles of common, everyday people with whom Jesus traveled. Finally, John devotes considerable energy to the relational aspects of our Christianity and how the events that took place reveal the character of God and shape our Theology. When the books were Canonized, they were put into this order because of those differences in each book's style. Matthew forms the bridge to the Old Testament, and then Mark puts that fulfillment into the moment and into action. Luke corroborates both accounts with facts and details. John is at the end because it was less integral with the other three and written much later. For those who have significant Bible knowledge as a basis, and for those who are making preparation to do an in-depth study of all John's literature, this is what I do recommend.

Traditional Harmony: In this approach, you read the longest or most detailed account of each story either solely or first, then read the other accounts for their added details or complementary differences. This is how I did it for several years whenever I re-read the accounts or led a group study. The trouble I had with this approach is that you sometimes end up reading only a few verses at a time from each account. It can make it tough to understand the context for each account and ends up losing so much focus on the overarching message of Jesus that you miss the primary lessons desired.

Interlinear Harmony: In this approach, you read "all the accounts at once." Without a study aid, this is extremely difficult. Even a 'side-by-side harmony' is tough to follow. One book on the market, <u>A Harmony of the Gospels</u> by Orville E. Daniel, does an excellent job at making this very do-able. In his harmony, Daniel puts all four accounts side by side, then boldfaces a text stream that captures every unique word and idea presented by the four accounts. For its intended purpose, this book and approach are exceptional. The trouble with this approach for our study is that you do get the primary lessons from each passage, but the contrast in this case is lost. You also do not have the opportunity to develop a feel for the intentional contrasts, nor the character of each book, and how those can help shape our understanding. Mr. Daniel's book is excellent, and I do recommend it for studies trying to understand the central core message of the Gospels, but we are looking for something different out of our current study.

Introductory Reading: In this approach, you read each Gospel as an entire book, but in a different order from the Canon. For someone who has limited or no knowledge of the Bible this can be the least confusing approach. I agree with many commentaries that strongly recommend not reading Matthew first. Matthew never intended to 'introduce' someone to Christ. Matthew's design was to 'prove' based on prior knowledge. The most common modified order I have seen is Mark, Matthew, Luke, then John. I have also seen Luke, Matthew, Mark, and John often. A few recent studies start with John, an approach I do not personally agree with. My personal recommendation for going through the Gospels with this method is Mark, Luke, Matthew, and then John. In fact, if you find that you simply cannot stand doing the reading schedule I recommend because reading harmonies just will not work with your learning style, I ask that you use this method. Read two chapters per day, five days per week, in the order Mark, Luke, Matthew, then John, and you will get some balance between the individual lessons presented and the contrast from each Gospel.

Simplified Harmony of the Gospels
Reading Schedule, WEEK ONE

Date of Sunday beginning

week of reading: _____

As each reading is completed,
write the date in the "Done"
column.

Done	Day	What	Read	Ct
	1	Jesus Before Time Began, Genealogy of Jesus, Mary & Joseph Betrothal, Jesus Born, Visit of the Magi, Flee to Egypt, Herod Kills Baby Boys	John 1:1-5 Matt 1:1-25 Matt 2:1-23	53
	2	Introduction, John the Baptizer Prophesied, Jesus' Birth Prophesied, Mary Stays with Elizabeth, Mary Gives Thanks, John is Born, Zacharias Prophesies	Luke 1:1-80	80
	3	Jesus Born, Jesus Presented at the Temple, Jesus in Nazareth and Visits to Jerusalem || John the Baptizer & his Witness of Christ	Luke 2:1-52 John 1:6-42	89

	4	John the Baptizer, Jesus' Baptism, Jesus Fasts & Temptation || John the Baptizer, Jesus' Baptism, Jesus Fasts & Temptation || John the Baptizer, Jesus' Baptism, Jesus Fasts & Temptation || Jesus' Early Public Ministry, Jesus Turns Water to Wine at Cana, First Passover of Public Ministry and First Cleansing of Temple	Luke 3:1-22 Luke 4:1-13 Mark 1:1-13 Matt 3:1-17 Matt 4:1-11 John 1:43-51 John 2:1-25	110
	5	Jesus Explains the New Birth to Nicodemus, John's Final Witness, Jesus' Early Judean Ministry & Return to Galilee, Samaritan Woman at the Well, Healing a Nobleman's Son	John 3:1-36 John 4:1-54	90
			Total Verses:	422

Simplified Harmony of the Gospels
Reading Schedule, WEEK TWO

Date of Sunday beginning

week of reading: _____

As each reading is completed,
write the date in the "Done"
column.

Done	Day	What	Read	Ct
	1	Healing at Bethesda, Jesus' Discourse on His Deity, Discourse on The Resurrection, Witness to Christ's Deity | | Jesus' Galilean Ministry, Jesus Heals Many, Heals the Paralytic, Calls Matthew, Discourse on the Sabbath, Heals on the Sabbath	John 5:1-47 Mark 1:14-45 Mark 2:1-28 Mark 3:1-12	119
	2	Organizes His Disciples, Parable of the Sower, Parable of the Soils, Explanation of the Parables, Parables of the Seeds, Jesus Stills the Sea, The Demoniac in the Tombs, Jesus Heals Woman with Hemorrhage, Raises Daughter of Synagogue Official from the Dead	Mark 3:13-35 Mark 4:1-41 Mark 5:1-43	107

	3	Teaches on His Own Rejection & Sends out The 12, John the Baptizer Dies, Jesus Feeds the Five Thousand, Jesus Walks on Water, Heals at Gennesaret || Jesus' Galilean Ministry, Early Disciples Called, Sermon on The Mount: Attitude; Discipleship	Mark 6:1-56 Matt 4:12-25 Matt 5:1-20	90
	4	Sermon on The Mount: Relationships; Giving; Prayer; Fasting; Service; True Confidence; Righteous Judgment; Prayer; Two Foundations	Matt 5:21-48 Matt 6:1-34 Matt 7:1-29	91
	5	Jesus Heals a Leper, Centurion of Great Faith, Peter's Mother-in-law Healed, Tests of Discipleship, Demoniac in the Tombs, Paralytic Healed, Discourse on Compassion || Jesus Raises Daughter of Synagogue Offical from the Dead, Heals Many Others	Matt 8:1-34 Matt 9:1-38	72
			Total Verses:	479

Simplified Harmony of the Gospels
Reading Schedule, WEEK THREE

Date of Sunday beginning
week of reading: _____

As each reading is completed,
write the date in the "Done"
column.

Done	Day	What	Read	Ct
	1	Sends out The 12, Discourses on Discipleship, John Asks Jesus for Reassurance and Receives It, Discourses on Rejection and Acceptance	Matt 10:1-42 Matt 11:1-30	72
	2	Discourse on the Sabbath, Jesus Heals on the Sabbath, Rebukes Pharisees, Speaks of Integrity, The Sign of Jonah, Relationships, Parable of the Soils and Explanation	Matt 12:1-50 Matt 13:1-23	73
	3	Parable of Tares, Parable of the Mustard Seed, Parable of the Leaven, Parable of Tares Explained, Hidden Treasure & Pearl of Great Price, Parable of Dragnet, Return to Nazareth, John the Baptizer Dies, Jesus Feeds	Matt 13:24-58 Matt 14:1-36	71

		Five Thousand, Jesus Walks on Water		
	4	Jesus' Galilean Ministry, Miraculous Catch of Fish, Peter's Mother-in-law Healed, Many Healed, Early Disciples, Heals a Leper, Heals a Paralytic, Discourse on Discipleship	Luke 4:14-44 Luke 5:1-39	70
	5	Discourse on the Sabbath, Jesus Heals on the Sabbath, Rebukes Pharisees, Sermon on The Mount: Attitude, Parables of Brotherhood and Two Foundations, Centurion of Great Faith, Jesus Reassures John, Pharisees Criticize Jesus, Sinful Woman Anoints Jesus' Feet With Tears, Parable of Two Debtors	Luke 6:1-49 Luke 7:1-50	99
			Total Verses:	385

Simplified Harmony of the Gospels
Reading Schedule, WEEK FOUR

Date of Sunday beginning

week of reading: _____

As each reading is completed,
write the date in the "Done"
column.

Done	Day	What	Read	Ct
	1	Christian Women, Parable of Soils, Parable of the Lamp, Jesus Calms the Sea, Demoniac in the Tombs, Jesus Raises Jairus' Daughter from The Dead, Heals the Woman with Hemorrhage, Sends out The 12, Jesus Feeds the Five Thousand, The Transfiguration, Jesus Heals a Demoniac	Luke 8:1-56 Luke 9:1-45	101
	2	Jesus' Discourse on Greatness, Discourse on the Demands of Discipleship || Jesus Feeds the Five Thousand, Jesus Walks on Water, Jesus' Discourse 'I Am The Bread Of Life", Peter's Statement of Loyalty	Luke 9:46-62 John 6:1-71	88

	3	Jesus' Discourse on Tradition versus Righteousness, Jesus Casts Out Demons, Heals Deaf-Mute Man, Jesus Feeds the Four Thousand, Peter's Great Declaration of Christ	Mark 7:1-37 Mark 8:1-38	75
	4	The Transfiguration, Jesus' Discourse on His Deity & Discipleship, Jesus Foretells His Death & Resurrection	Mark 9:1-50	50
	5	Jesus' Discourse on Tradition versus Righteousness, Jesus Casts Out Demons, Heals Many, Jesus Feeds the Four Thousand,, Pharisees Ask for Sign, Peter's Great Declaration of Christ, Jesus Foretells His Death, Jesus Discourse on the Cost of Discipleship	Matt 15:1-39 Matt 16:1-28	67
			Total Verses:	381

Simplified Harmony of the Gospels
Reading Schedule, WEEK FIVE
Date of Sunday beginning
week of reading: _____
As each reading is completed,
write the date in the "Done"
column.

Done	Day	What	Read	Ct
	1	The Transfiguration, Jesus Casts Demons Out of Boy, Discourse on Faith, Predicts His Death, Coin From Fishes' Mouth, Discourses on First In the Kingdom & Caution With Liberty, The Lost Sheep, Discipline & Prayer, Discourse on Forgiveness	Matt 17:1-27 Matt 18:1-35	62
	2	The Seventy Disciples Sent Out, Results of Evangelism, Parable of The Good Samaritan, Jesus, Martha & Mary, Jesus Teaches Disciples to Pray, Pharisees Blaspheme & Jesus' Discourse on Unified Evangelism, The Sign of Jonah	Luke 10:1-42 Luke 11:1-36	78

	3	Jesus Chastises Hypocrisy of the Pharisees & Promises His, God's and Holy Spirit Support for the Righteous, Parable of Rich Man Building Bigger Barns, Discourse on True Riches, Warning to Be Prepared, Discourse on Possible Division For Sake of Righteousness	Luke 11:37-54 Luke 12:1-12 Luke 12:13-59	77
	4	Parable of Fig Tree That Did Not Bear Fruit & Call To Repentance, Jesus Heals Woman Sick With a Spirit on the Sabbath, Parables of the Mustard Seed & Leaven || Jesus' Discourse at the Feast of Booths On: Righteous Unity, His Unity With the Father, Righteous Works, Belief In Him; The People Divided Over Jesus	Luke 13:1-21 John 7:1-53	74
	5	Woman Caught in Act of Adultery, Jesus' Discourse on Light & Life, Jesus' Discourse on Truth Will Make You Free, Jesus Heals the Man Born Blind	John 8:1-59 John 9:1-41	100
			Total Verses:	391

Simplified Harmony of the Gospels
Reading Schedule, WEEK SIX
Date of Sunday beginning
week of reading: _____
As each reading is completed,
write the date in the "Done"
column.

Done	Day	What	Read	Ct
	1	Parable of the Good Shepherd & Discourse on Jesus' Deity | | Jesus Teaches on Divorce, Jesus Blesses the Children, The Rich Young Ruler, Jesus Foretells His Death, Jesus Heals Bartimaeus' Sight	John 10:1-39 Mark 10:1-52	91
	2	Jesus Teaches on Divorce, Jesus Blesses the Children, The Rich Young Ruler, Jesus Promises the Disciples their Reward, Parable of the Laborers in the Vineyard, Jesus Foretells His Resurrection, James and John's Mother asks for Preferential Treatment, Jesus Heals Two Blind Men	Matt 19:1-30 Matt 20:1-34	64

	3	Jesus' Discourse on the Cost of Discipleship & Mourns Jerusalem, Jesus Heals on the Sabbath, Parable of the Guests, Parable of the Dinner, Cost of Discipleship, Parables of the Lost Sheep, Lost Coin, and Lost Son	Luke 13:22-35 Luke 14:1-35 Luke 15:1-32	81
	4	Parable of the Unrighteous Steward, Parable of the Rich Man and Lazarus, Jesus' Discourse on Righteous Discipleship, Jesus Foretells His Second Coming	Luke 16:1-31 Luke 17:1-37	68
	5	Parable of the Importunate Widow, Parable of the Pharisee and the Publican, Jesus' Discussion with the Rich Young Ruler, Jesus Heals Bartimaeus' Sight, Jesus Disciples Zaccheus, Parable of Good Stewardship (Talents)	Luke 18:1-43 Luke 19:1-27	27
			Total Verses:	374

Simplified Harmony of the Gospels
Reading Schedule, WEEK SEVEN

Date of Sunday beginning
week of reading: _____

As each reading is completed, write the date in the "Done" column.

Done	Day	What	Read	Ct
	1	Jesus Raises Lazarus From the Dead, Pharisees Persecute Jesus to the Point He Goes to Ephraim	John 10:40-42 John 11:1-57	60
	2	Jesus' Triumphal Entry Into Jerusalem, Jesus Cleanses the Temple, Jesus' Authority Questioned, Parable of the Vine-growers, Paying Tribute to Caesar, The Resurrection	Luke 19:28-48 Luke 20:1-47	68
	3	The Widow's Two Lepta, Jesus' Discourse to Take Courage; Trials are Necessary Before His Return, Preparing the Passover, Instituting the Lord's Supper, Who Is Greatest	Luke 21:1-38 Luke 22:1-38	76

	4	Jesus in Gethsemane, Jesus Arrested, Jesus Before The Sanhedrin, Then Pilate, Then Herod, Then Pilate Again: Jesus Crucified and Buried	Luke 22:39-71 Luke 23:1-56	89
	5	The Triumphal Entry, Jesus Cleanses the Temple, Jesus' Authority Questioned, Parable of the Vineyard Workers, Discourse on Paying Tribute to Caesar, The Authority of Christ, The Widow's Mite	Mark 11:1-33 Mark 12:1-44	44
			Total Verses:	370

Simplified Harmony of the Gospels
Reading Schedule, WEEK EIGHT

Date of Sunday beginning

week of reading: _____

As each reading is completed,
write the date in the "Done"
column.

Done	Day	What	Read	Ct
	1	Discourse on Necessary Trials to Come Before Jesus' Return, Woman Anoints Jesus With Nard, The Last Passover, The Lord's Supper Instituted, Jesus in Gethsemane & Arrest	Mark 13:1-36 Mark 14:1-52	88
	2	Jesus Before the Sanhedrin, Peter's Three Denials, Jesus Before Pilate, Jesus Mocked & Beaten, Jesus Crucified & Buried	Mark 14:53-72 Mark 15:1-47	67
	3	The Triumphal Entry, Jesus Cleanses the Temple, Jesus Withers the Barren Fig Tree, Jesus Asserts His Authority, Parable of the Two Sons, Parable of the Landowner, Parable of the Marriage Feast, Jesus on Paying Tribute to Caesar, Jesus Answers the Sadducees Regarding the Resurrection, Jesus on The Greatest Command	Matt 21:1-46 Matt 22:1-46	92

	4	Jesus on the Hypocrisy of the Pharisees & Seven Woes to Scribes, Pharisees, and Hypocrites; Jesus Laments Jerusalem, Jesus Foretells Destruction of the Temple, Discourse on Necessary Trials to Come Before Jesus' Return, Jesus on His Return, Parable of the Fig Tree, Be Prepared	Matt 23:1-39 Matt 24:1-51	90
	5	Parable of the Ten Virgins, Parable of the Talents, Jesus' Discourse on the Judgment, Woman Anoints Jesus with Perfume, Judas Makes His Bargain, The Last Passover, The Lord's Supper Instituted, Jesus in Gethsemane, Jesus Betrayal & Arrest	Matt 25:1-46 Matt 26:1-56	102
			Total Verses:	439

Simplified Harmony of the Gospels
Reading Schedule, WEEK NINE

Date of Sunday beginning

week of reading: _____

As each reading is completed, write

the date in the "Done" column.

Done	Day	What	Read	Ct
	1	Jesus Before Caiaphas & Sanhedrin, Peter's Three Denials, Judas' Remorse, Jesus Before Pilate, Jesus Mocked & Beaten, Jesus Crucified & Buried	Matt 26:57-68 Matt 27:1-66	78
	2	Mary Anoints Jesus with Nard, The Triumphal Entry, Jesus' Discourse on His Coming Death & Righteous Discipleship, The Lord's Supper, Jesus Washes the Disciples Feet, Jesus Speaks of His Betrayal & Righteous Discipleship	John 12:1-50 John 13:1-38	88

	3	Jesus Comforts His Disciples, Jesus' Unity with the Father, Jesus on the Role of the Spirit, Jesus on Obedience & Righteousness, Jesus' "I am the Vine", Disciples' Relationships With One Another & The World, Jesus Warns of Trials & Promises the Holy Spirit	John 14:1-31 John 15:1-27 John 16:1-15	73
	4	Jesus Foretells His Death & Resurrection, Instruction on Prayer & Warnings of Coming Persecution, Jesus Prays, Jesus Prays the Disciples, Jesus Prays for the Disciples' Glory, Jesus Arrested, Jesus Before Annas, Then Caiaphas, Peter's Denial of Jesus, Jesus Before Pilate	John 16:16-33 John 17:1-26 John 18:1-40	84
	5	Jesus Scourged & Mocked, Jesus Crucified & Burial	John 19:1-42	42
			Total Verses:	365

Simplified Harmony of the Gospels
Reading Schedule, WEEK TEN

Date of Sunday beginning
week of reading: _____

As each reading is completed,
write the date in the "Done"
column.

Done	Day	What	Read	Ct
	1	Jesus' Resurrection, The Great Commission	Mark 16:1-20	20
	2	Jesus' Resurrection, The Great Commission, Jesus' Ascension	Matt 28:1-20	20
	3	Jesus' Resurrection, Jesus & Disciples on Road to Emmaus, Jesus' Final Discourse with Disciples, Jesus' Ascension	Luke 24:1-53	53
	4	Jesus' Resurrection, Jesus Appears to the Twelve & Disciples, Jesus Appears in Galilee, Miraculous Catch of Fish, Jesus Discourse "Feed My Sheep", Jesus' Final Discourse	John 20:1-31 John 21:1-25	56

Total Verses: 149

Simplified Harmony

There are many harmony texts and tables available today. Many are excellent and responsible in their approach to harmonizing the events recorded in the Gospel accounts. Most break down the life of Jesus into more detail than we need. The typical 'other choice' is to break Jesus' life into the first, second, and third years of His ministry.

I like to break the life of Christ into 14 segments & milestones. For some of the time periods, I have chosen traditional titles based on where Jesus spent His time. For example, what is the start of Jesus' second year of ministry lasting into his third year took place primarily in Galilee; therefore, I named those two years "Jesus' Galilean Ministry." Where I have departed from some traditional tables is giving equal visibility to some of the shorter regional visits Jesus made, for example, the month Jesus spent in Sychar and Samaria before His Galilean Ministry in the segment "Jesus' Visit to Samaria."

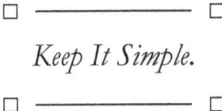

Keep It Simple.

Refer to this table from time to time as you read. You may find you keep your bearings better regarding 'where' those events are taking place, and 'when' those events fall relative to the balance of the Gospel account.

What	When	How Long	Where	Matthew	Mark	Luke	John
Jesus Before Time Began	Everywhen	Forever	Everywhere				John 1:1-3
Jesus' Birth, Childhood	~ 5 BC	~30 Years	Bethlehem, Egypt, Galilee	Matt 1-2		Luke 1-2	
John the Baptizer	25 AD	2 Years		Matt 3:1-12	Mark 1:1-8	Luke 3:1-20	John 1:6-42
Jesus' Baptism	27 AD		Jordan River south of Nazareth	Matt 3:13-17	Mark 1:9-11	Luke 3:21-22	
Jesus Fasts & Tempted	27 AD	40 Days	Wilderness Near Galilee	Matt 4:1-11	Mark 1:12-13	Luke 4:1-13	
Jesus' Pre-Ministry Miracle	Spring 27 AD	1 Week	Cana in Galilee				John 2:1-11
Jesus' Early Judean Ministry	Summer 27 AD	2 Months	Judea				John 2:13-4:3

What	When	How Long	Where	Matthew	Mark	Luke	John
Jesus' Visit to Samaria	Summer 27 AD	1 Month	Sychar, Samaria				John 4:4-42
Jesus' Galilean Ministry	Late 27 AD	2 Years	Galilee	Matt 4:12-19:1	Mark 1:14-10:1	Luke 4:14-9:62	John 4:43-54 & John 6
Jesus' Visit to Jerusalem	Galilean Ministry spring 28 AD	Uncertain ~ 1 Month?	Jerusalem				John 5:1-47
Jesus' Later Judean Ministry	Summer/Fall 29 AD	1 Month	Judea (Bethany, Perea)			Luke 10:1-13:21	John 7:1-10:39
Jesus' Perean Ministry	Winter 29 to Spring 30 AD	4 Months	Perea (& Judea)	Matt 19:1-20:34	Mark 10:1-52	Luke 13:22-19:27	John 10:40-11:57
Jesus' Last Week & Crucifixion	April, 30 AD	1 Week	Judea, Jerusalem	Matt 21-27	Mark 11-15	Luke 19:28-24:1	John 12-19
Jesus' Appearances after Rising	Late Spring 30 AD	40 Days	Jerusalem, Galilee	Matt 28	Mark 16	Luke 24	John 20-21

The Disciple John Mark

No study of the disciple John Mark is complete without studying his mother, Mary. The only way to truly understand and appreciate Mark is by looking to Mary first. Having a mother who was able to shape the path and progress of the early Church left an unmistakable and indelible impression on Mark. Inasmuch as I am able, we will take them together, focusing first on Mary, then spend our energies on Mark.

Mary, as the most substantive point of Biblical history, is the mother of John Mark, a man who became indispensable to Paul in his ministry (1 Tim 4:11). This alone would set her apart from most women in history; her ability to raise a man with such immense potential.

In addition to her physical motherly virtue, she gave to many of the early Christians as if they were her own flesh and blood. Because John Mark is traditionally ascribed as one of the 70 disciples commissioned by, and who often traveled with, Jesus (Luke 10:1-37, Acts 1:21), it is logical to believe that his mother Mary would have been in frequent contact with him as well. Early tradition ascribes the 'upper room' where Jesus held his last supper to being in Mary's house (Mark 14:13-16). We know that Peter saw Mary's home as a place where he could seek comfort and refuge (Acts 12).

This makes sense, as Mark records more detail about the house than any other gospel writer; he could have lived there. This same house is where the Apostles gathered following Jesus' crucifixion and were commissioned by Jesus (Mark 16:14-18, John 20:19-29). This is consistent, as the Apostles would have had no where else to go, but to the house of one of the 70, John Mark. Early texts attest that it was that same house that the early church used as a base (Acts 1:12-14).

Later, it is certain that the Christians at Jerusalem used her house as a meeting place (Acts 12:12-19). Peter's first thought was likely to reach James, Elder of the church at Jerusalem, whom he expected to find at Mary's house. It is a true testimonial to this woman that Peter's first thought after God liberated him from prison was to reach her home. It is also possible that the church meeting for the Jerusalem Council took place at Mary's house (Acts 14:27 - 15:29).

If we were to select a verse that most strongly characterizes Mary as a person, I personally choose:

> **"And when he realized this, he went to the house of Mary, the mother of John who was also called Mark, where many were gathered together and were praying."**
>
> **(NASV, Acts 12:12)**

Mary was wealthier than the average person. She clearly owned her own home and was able to lend support to both the Church through meetings in that home and to the Apostles, like Peter, when they had no other place to go. From her home being open to the prayer vigil previously mentioned, we gain insight into her being generous with those physical blessings. We also know that Mary had a servant girl named Rhoda (Acts 12:14), which further supports the idea that Mary was well-off.

We also know that Mary must have been a sister, sister-in-law, or aunt to Barnabas (Acts 12:12, Col 4:10). Barnabas was a key figure in early Church history and missions in his own right. This entire family was active in the spread of the Gospel and well-known in the Christian community.

Much of what we assume to be true about Mary comes to us also from the Apostolic fathers and secular histories. St. Jerome, translator of the Latin Vulgate Bible, ascribes John Mark as being one of the 70 commissioned by Jesus in Luke 10. His writings in the 4th century references 2nd century writings to that effect.

The Syrian Orthodox Bishopric headquarters is on the site they hold Mary's house originally stood, according to their 3rd century texts.

Writings from the Syrian liturgy dating back to the 4th century claim that Mary was known by name as far away as Syria and Cyprus.

Bishop Epiphanius, a native of Palestine, wrote in the 4th century, referring to 2nd century works: 'Hadrian...found the whole city razed to the ground and the Temple of God destroyed... ...only a few houses were standing and the House of God (church house) was... ... a little building... ...same place as the Upper Room. This (church) was built... ...home of a Christian (Mary of Jerusalem, mother of the Hammer, John Mark) was left standing until the time of Emperor Constantine.'

St. Cyril of Jerusalem, in 348 AD, refers to the 'Upper Church of the Apostles where the Holy Spirit descended upon them' in the same context as "...where Peter sought solace."

The Spanish Nun Aetheria, in 385 AD, named the site of Mary's house as the scene of both the resurrection appearance of Jesus and the events at Pentecost. She described the special services held in this church on these great festivals, as well as the prayer vigils this house was 'well known for.'

The pilgrim Theodosius, in 530 AD, adds the fact that the Upper Room was in the house of 'Mark the Evangelist'. He also calls the house of the Upper Room 'the first

Synagogue of the Church and their headquarters in Jerusalem.'

With such an undeniable heritage shaping the Church, it is no wonder John, also called Mark, entered missions with Paul and Barnabas. It is also easier for us to now understand why Mark has such a capacity for excitement in the writing of his Gospel, and why there must have been enormous pressure on him.

As a young man he began following Christ and the disciples and was eager to do the right thing. At Jesus' arrest, authorities seized a young man who then fled naked, leaving his clothes behind (Mark 14:50-51). This is the only figure left in anonymity in Mark's account of the Gospel, so it is not too great a leap to accept the early tradition that this was Mark himself. This is just after his disciples had vowed never to leave Jesus (Mark 14:31). John Mark later started the First Missionary Journey with Paul and Barnabas only to desert them in Paphos, Cyprus (Acts 13:13). Paul and Barnabas had a sharp disagreement and parted company over whether to take him on the Second Missionary Journey (Acts 15:37-39).

In the year following, John Mark highly likely authored the book of Mark. He was in, or on his way to, Rome during the writing of the book. Some believe that Peter was with him during the writing of the book. Later Mark went with Barnabas to Cyprus to support the Christians there (Acts 15:39). Although he deserted Paul and Barnabas during the first missionary journey, and fled Jesus side during Jesus' arrest, John Mark in later years grew to be a highly regarded mission worker. Paul mentions him in most grateful and appreciative terms (Col. 4:10-11), as being a "fellow worker" (Philemon 24), and "helpful to me in my ministry" (2 Tim. 4:11).

As you have read, John Mark had made some mistakes in the beginning of his life, but through encouragement and patience from Barnabas, he was able to overcome and learn from his mistakes. Mistakes are effective teachers. Their consequences have a way of making lessons painfully clear. If we learn from our mistakes, we are likely to develop wisdom, as John Mark did.

If I select a verse that characterizes Mark, it would be:

> **"Only Luke is with me. Get Mark and bring him with you because he is helpful to me in my ministry."**
>
> **(NIV, 2 Tim 4:11)**

Mark died in Alexandria, of a martyr's death, according to tradition. The Bible never mentions his father, implying that he was either a non-believer or had passed away. We cannot know for sure. Mark's given birth name was John, which is a Jewish name meaning 'God is Gracious' (Acts

12:12, 25). It was standard practice for Jews to receive or adopt a proper Roman name that was more familiar to Latin speakers. It was this adult name, either taken or given when Mark began to travel, that was Marcus, meaning 'Large Hammer' (Acts 12:12 & 25). He served in an invaluable role by supporting missions as an assistant (Acts 13:5) and was himself a minister of the word (Luke 1:2). History credits him with establishing churches in Alexandria, as cited by Eusebius in his writings of Ecclesiastical History.

What lessons can we then take from his life? Certainly, we should learn that personal maturity often stems from a combination of time and experience, including the lessons learned from mistakes. Mistakes are not as important as learning from them. In life, measure your success not by what you accomplish, but by what you overcome to accomplish it. Encouragement can change a person's life.

The Gospel of Mark

What:

The Gospel According to Mark.

Why:

Present the person, work, and teachings of Jesus with emphasis on action. "Jesus the Servant" (Mark 10:42-45).

When:

AD 50.

Evidence exists for Mark's writing between AD 50 and AD 65. Mark's use of language reflected later in Peter's letters strongly supports these dates (Mark 10:45, 1 Peter 5:13). History places them both at Rome around AD 50 to AD 60. Due to its flavor of action, many believe it to be a gospel written with a sense of urgency - supporting an early date. For this study, we will agree with that early date of AD 50.

Where:

Rome. John Mark was there following the completion of Paul's first missionary journey.

From Who:

John Mark. Although not one of the 12 disciples, he went with Paul on his first missionary journey (Acts 13:13), and was known for his role in the first century church (2 Tim 4:11).

To Whom:

John Mark recorded the life of Jesus for the Christians at Rome. Indeed, Mark targeted his Gospel at those who had limited understanding of Judaism (Mark 7:3-4; 12:18). He translates several Aramaic expressions for those more familiar with Greek, further showing that Mark is trying to include non-Hebrew readers in the Good News of Jesus Christ (Mark 5:41; 7:11, 34; 15:22). The absence of a genealogy in this early treatise has on Jesus' life also points to a non-Jewish audience.

Setting:

> The Roman Empire under Tiberius
> Caesar. The empire had a universal
> language and an excellent road system.
> These, in combination with the zeal of the
> 1st century church, made the time ideal for
> the spread of the gospel.

Key Verse:

> **"For even the son of man did not come to
> be served, but to serve, and to give his life
> a ransom for many."**
>
> **(NASV: Mark 10:45)**

Distinguishing Characteristics:

It was the first gospel recorded and one of the first three
books of the New Testament. The other three gospels
quote all but 31 verses of the Gospel of Mark. Mark
records 18 miracles of Jesus, a relatively large number
considering the length of this book in comparison with
the other Gospel accounts (1:23-27, 29-31, 40-45; 2:1-12;
3:1-5; 4:35-44; 5:1-20, 25-34, 35-43; 6:35-44; 45-52; 7:24-
30, 31-37; 8:1-9, 22-26; 9:14-29; 10:46-52; 11:12-24). In
contrast, Mark records only 4 parables (Soils 4:2-8,
Growing Wheat 4:26-29, Mustard Seed 4:30-32, Wicked
Tenants 12:1-9), the fewest of the synoptic gospels.

The Gospel of Mark portrays a sense of urgency, characterized by quick movement, activity, rapidity, and impulsiveness. Many attribute the Apostle Peter with exercising a lot of influence on John Mark, and on how he recorded this Gospel. Internal evidence also shows that John Mark relied on Peter. There is an interesting first-person reference to Peter speaking (Mark 11:21), and other allusions to Peter participating as the storyteller (Mark 1:36; 14:37; 16:7).

This gospel is also known for its vividness of detail. Mark uses descriptive colors ('...green grass...,' Mark 6:39), and full descriptions of action taking place ('...immediately the spirit threw him... ...falling... ... rolling about and foaming at the mouth.', Mark 9:20). Interestingly, Mark also records facial expressions, interprets emotions of onlookers, and some private remarks: '...laughed him to scorn...' (5:40), '...his countenance fell...' (10:22), '...were amazed...were afraid...' (10:32), '...moved with indignation...' (10:41), '...reasoned with themselves...' (11:31), '...their eyes were very heavy..." (14:40).

Mark omits all but one of the longer discourses by Jesus, the Olivet Discourse (Mark 13). He emphasizes the actions, rather than the words, of Christ. In so doing, he pauses only long enough to explain certain Jewish customs to his Roman audience. In a similar vein he quotes the Old Testament least of the gospels and never mentions the word 'law.' (Matthew mentions 'law' eight times, Luke nine times, and John fifteen.)

Mark's Gospel has many Semitic idioms and constructions that reflect its underlying Hebrew/Aramaic background, allowing Mark to convey complex theological and cultural concepts with remarkable economy of language. These "Latinisms" (in the broader sense of condensed, meaning-packed expressions) show Mark's ability to compress layers of significance into brief, memorable phrases. Clear examples of Semitic idioms in Mark include:

- "Sons of thunder" (Mark 3:17) - Boanerges. The "son of…" construction (bar/ben) is distinctly Semitic, used to describe character traits or associations.
- "Out of the heart" (Mark 7:21) - "From within, out of the heart of men, proceed evil thoughts…" The heart as the seat of moral decision-making is a Hebrew idiom.
- "It would be good for that man if he had never been born" (Mark 14:21) - A Semitic way of expressing the ultimate misfortune or curse.
- Pleonastic "answered and said" - Throughout Mark, this redundant construction mirrors Hebrew narrative style (wayya'an wayyo'mer).

- "Amen, I say to you" - Jesus's signature phrase uses the Hebrew liturgical formula in an unprecedented way.
- Preserved Aramaic phrases - Talitha cumi, Ephphatha, Abba - direct cultural transfers that pack specific meaning.

This evidence suggests Mark thinks in distinctly Semitic patterns while writing in Greek. However, rather than simply translating, Mark is consciously crafting a narrative that bridges cultural worlds; Mark employs clear Greek syntax and vocabulary alongside these Semitic idioms to make his message accessible to both Jewish and Gentile audiences. His word choices reflect his theological mission: creating a Gospel that honors its Hebrew roots while staying comprehensible across cultural boundaries.

Although a synoptic gospel, Mark omits a lot of historical detail in favor of detail of the moment. He makes no reference to Jesus' genealogy or childhood. The focus is on Jesus' humanity and His service in the role of 'being human.' Mark calls Him a 'Son of Man' at least 13 times in this Gospel (2:10, 28; 8:31, 38; 9:9, 12, 31; 10:33, 45; 13:26; 14:21, 41, 62).

Mark gives exceptional insight into what motivated Jesus' actions: '…moved with compassion…' (1:41), '…looked around with anger…grieved…' (3:5), '…perceiving it…' (8:17), '…leave her alone…' (14:6), '…sorely troubled…'

(14:33). It is in the context of those emotions motivating Jesus in His humanity that Mark holds to Jesus on a personal level. Mark ensures Jesus' humanity is ever known: '...His friends...said, He is beside Himself.' (3:21), '...asleep...' (4:38), with family and disappointment with His countrymen (6:3-6), '...the hour no one knows...neither the Son...' (13:32)

Notable Lessons:

All of Mark's lessons center on the humanity and servanthood of Christ.

1. Jesus Christ alone is the Son of God. Jesus performs miracles only explicable by His deity and does so in contexts only explainable by His humanity. (Mark 1:25-26, 3:5,16:6, 10:45)

2. Jesus came to earth as a servant. Jesus was selfless and self-depreciating. Compassion motivated Jesus above everything else (1:41) and He showed it in His servitude (10:45).

3. Jesus is a man of action. Jesus used words only to explain His actions, giving him the opportunity to bring others into contact with Him (7:32-37).

4. The gospel must be spread to all. Jesus only formally commissioned his followers to convert the Jews during His life, then broadened that commission prior to ascension to include all men, but it is clear from Jesus' actions that this Great Commission was on His heart all the time (7:25-30; 16:15)

Outline:

A. Birth and Preparation of Jesus, the Servant (1:1-13)

    1. The ministry of John (1:1-8)

    2. The Baptism of Jesus (1:9-11)

    3. Temptation of Jesus (1:12-23)

B. The ministry of Jesus

    1. The Galilean Ministry (1:14 - 9:50)

        a. First Period: Gathering disciples, healing the paralytic, the Sabbath (1:14 - 3:12)

        b. Second Period: Friends or Foes, Parables, First Withdrawal, Rejection, Mission

The Disciple Luke

Luke seems to appear as if from nowhere near the beginning of Paul's Second Missionary Journey (Acts 16:10). Even this involvement is only implied by the change of pronouns from 'they' to 'we.' Most people know that Luke was a doctor, and that he wrote the Gospel of Luke and the Acts of the Apostles. Some even realize that he was a Gentile.

How do we make the leap from a Gentile doctor who does not appear to come on the scene until about 50 A.D. to a man with such irrefutable first-hand knowledge that he is a trusted Gospel chronicler? Is our perception of Luke an accurate one?

First, the idea that a person had to be a first-hand witness to write a Gospel is a requirement of our own imagination. Luke himself says in the first few verses of his Gospel that he is putting together, in order, those stories 'we' have heard from those who actually saw it. Second, we have limited information written about Luke, but that in no way implies he is insufficient to the task at hand. While only mentioned by name three times in the New Testament (Col 4:14, 2 Tim 4:11, Phim 1:24), his writings more than pass the tests of time, consistency, accuracy, and comparative scrutiny.

Provided we understand what Paul implies in the closing to his letter to the Church at Colossae, we can confirm that Luke is a gentile. Paul lists those coworkers who are 'of circumcision,' then lists those he implies are not of circumcision. Luke is in the second list (Col 4:10-14). It is also from this passage that we know Luke was a physician. Paul's use of the term 'beloved' seems to imply that Luke not only was loved by Paul but was lovable to many in the work (Col 4:14).

Paul considered Luke a worker in the ministry, implying more than his roles as historian and doctor (Phim 1:24). It is also clear that Luke stood by Paul, even to the point of accompanying him to prison. Even when all others either chose or were forced to leave Paul's side, Luke remained (2 Tim 4:11).

Luke was the writer of two New Testament books, the Gospel of Luke and the book of Acts. Luke's writings comprise approximately 27% of the New Testament. Luke was an earnest disciple and showed a great deal of interest in the background, formation, and development of the early church. He traveled with Paul on his second and third missionary journeys and his trip to Rome (Acts 16:10-17; 20:5-15; 27:1-37; 28:1-14; 2 Tim 4:11).

Luke, in his writing of the Gospel of Luke and the book of Acts, was concerned that his writings provide a highly credible and historical account of Christian origins. His reference of events in Roman history illustrates this (Luke 2:1, 3:1-2, Acts 10:1, 11:19, 26:26). Luke made it clear in his writings that Christianity must be understood within the context of Jewish and Roman history. His attention to historical detail is unparalleled. As these accounts make no mention of the death of Paul, both Luke and Acts were likely complete and in circulation before Paul's death (64 A.D.).

In his writings, Luke specifically addresses Theophilus and also addresses Gentiles and people everywhere. There are many possibilities for who Theophilus is. The name means literally 'friend of God.' It is possible this is a specific person, either named Theophilus or nicknamed that by Luke, though if that is the case we have no clue about their identity otherwise. Many commentaries have suggested that this letter was written generically to 'all those who are friends of God.' Either is possible.

Traditional history suggests that Luke may have been from Antioch, although the evidence is scant at best. It could make sense, as Luke specifically calls out the city of Antioch many times in his writings (Acts 11:19-27; 13:1-3; 14:26; 15:22, 35; 18:22). Regardless of Luke's original hometown, we do know that he considered Philippi his home. He chose to remain behind in Philippi when Paul went to Corinth (Acts 16:40).

Paul considered Luke as 'highly valuable', lending guidance to the church at Philippi, acting as a physician, recording the longest Gospel account, and doing it all in relative anonymity. If I were to select a verse to sum up Luke as a person, it would be the verse he wrote to sum up his gospel account:

> **"Many have undertaken to draw up an account of the things that have been fulfilled among us, just as they were handed down to us by those who from the first were eyewitnesses and servants of the word. Therefore, since I myself have carefully investigated everything from the beginning, it seemed good also to me to write an orderly account for you, most excellent Theophilus, so that you may know the certainty of the things you have been taught."**
>
> **(NIV, Luke 1:1-4)**

Luke lived a life in which he was keenly aware of who he was, even if we sometimes overlook it. He understood that the words we use, and the legacy we leave, will become a picture of who we are. Luke knew that Paul was an intelligent and self-sufficient man. He also knew that no matter how successful Paul may be, he needed someone to come alongside him and support his work. Luke also knew that his training as a physician did not preclude him from serving others.

The Gospel of Luke

What:

The Gospel According to Luke.

Why:

To present an accurate account of the life of Christ, with emphasis on the facts of his perfection, both as a human and as the Savior (Luke 1:1-4). Luke expends extraordinary energy to show the value of those who are lost or currently outside the salvation of Christ (Luke 15). "Jesus the Savior of the Lost and Rejected."

When:

AD 58.

There are several possible dates for this book, but they fall into 2 groups: before Paul's death or after. Luke showed no sense of urgency in this record. Its language shows experienced reflection, indicating that Luke had already been through a great deal, but does not foresee imminent doom. This comes out in his writing about Jesus' preparation (Luke 4:17-21). For these reasons, in this study, we will agree with the earlier date of 58 AD, and a writing location of Caesarea.

Where:

Caesarea. Another possible location is Rome. Either location would have been during Luke's travel toward Paul's imprisonment in Rome – either his prison stays at Caesarea in 57 AD or in Rome in 60 AD. (Note that it is also likely the Acts of the Apostles was completed very shortly after this Gospel, and the two were likely circulated initially as a book pair 'Luke-Acts'.)

From Who:

Luke, who was a Greek doctor (Col 4:14), and a trusted companion to Paul (2 Tim 4:11). He is the only known Gentile writer in the New Testament.

To Whom:

Theophilus ("one who loves God"), and those who love God everywhere. Luke's Gospel appeals specifically to those who were introduced to God's word late; in other words, the Gentiles, and those who denied Him early in life.

Setting:

The Roman Empire under Nero (54 to 68 AD). The empire had a universal language and an excellent road system. Luke probably planned to use their upcoming trip to Rome as a mechanism to spread his record and therefore took great care in its content and phraseology.

Key Verse:

> *"And Jesus said to him, "Today salvation has come to this house, because he, too, is a son of Abraham. For the Son of Man has come to seek and to save that which was lost.""*
>
> *(NASV: Luke 19:9-10)*

Distinguishing Characteristics:

The single most identifiable characteristic about Luke's Gospel is his attention to fullness. It is the most comprehensive telling of Christ's life among the Gospels. Also, its general structure, in both vocabulary and composition, show that the author was a highly educated individual.

Only Luke recounts the angel Gabriel's announcement to Mary that she would conceive a child, born of God, who would be Messiah (Luke 1:26-38). Only Luke tells us of the Miraculous Catch of Fish that preceded Jesus calling some of His first Apostles (Luke 5:1-11). Luke makes this effort on fullness and accuracy felt throughout his account.

Luke makes several references to illnesses and diagnoses. He also pays special attention to distinguishing between those who are simply sick (Luke 4:38-40; 5:12-13), those who are dead (Luke 7:12-17), and those who are possessed with demons (Luke 8:27ff).

Luke stresses Jesus' relationships with people around him. He also portrays Jesus' desire to save all people regardless of race (Luke 1:13; 2:20; 9:51-56), sinfulness (Luke 2:32; 3:6-38; 7:37-50), or wealth (Luke 1:53; 19:2; 23:50). Likewise, Luke gives stronger attention to Jesus' relationships with women than do the other Gospels (Luke 8:1-3; 10:38-42). Many commentaries attribute this to his educated enlightenment and the strong possibility that he was of Greek descent.

One lengthy passage, from Luke 9:51 to Luke 18:35, contains information largely absent from the other Gospels. This section contains the familiar teachings of Jesus on the lost sheep, the lost coin, and the lost son (Luke 15). It also includes the description of the nine ungrateful lepers, and the one grateful one (Luke 17:11-19).

Luke contains 3 parables not grouped in the other Gospels The Lost Sheep, The Lost Coin, and the Lost Son (Luke 15); Luke also records more of Jesus' individual prayers than the other Gospels (Luke 5:16; 6:12; 9:28-29; 11:1-13; 18:1-14; 22:32, 44; 23:46).

Luke, likewise, records 20 miracles performed by Jesus. It appears that six unique to his Gospel, though not unique in terms of type of miracle. He records the Miraculous Catch of Fish preceding Jesus Ministry (Luke 5:1-11), while John records a similar miracle following Jesus' resurrection (John 21:1-14). He also records Jesus Raising the Son of a Widow at Nain (Luke 7:11-17), and calls to Jesus' compassion on the woman, knowing she was widowed, and this was her only son; few contest this miracle as a compassionate foreshadowing of Jesus own pending passion. He healed a woman on the Sabbath (Luke 13:10-17), a man with dropsy (Luke 14:1-6) and Healed Ten Lepers (Luke 17:11-19). Also, while other accounts record that Malchus, servant to the High Priest, had his ear cut off at Jesus' arrest, only Luke tells us that Jesus healed him (Luke 22:49-51). Interestingly, Luke omits the account of Jesus walking on water (Matt 14:22-33; Mark 6:45-52; John 6:15-21).

Luke also records many parables of Jesus, of which at least 10 are unique to Luke. The most notable of these unique parables include The Parable of the Good Samaritan (Luke 10:25-37), The Parable of the

Corrupt/Unjust Steward (Luke 16:1-12), and the Parables of the Lost Sheep, Lost Coin, and Prodigal Son (Luke 15). Other parables certainly unique to Luke include The Two Debtors, The Persistent Neighbor, The Rich Fool, The Barren Fig Tree, The Rich Man and Lazarus, The Master and Servant, The Importunate Widow, The Pharisee and the Publican (7:41-47; 11:5-8; 12:16-21; 13:6-9; 16:19-31; 17:7-10; 18:1-8; 18:9-14). Where Luke does record the same parable as other Gospel accounts, and where those records include details not included by the other writers, those added details are invariably on behalf of the lost, the poor, the rejected, or the destitute.

Notable Lessons:

There are several complementary facets of Jesus' life that Luke wants us to see. Luke's themes are not grouped by topic, so they are often hard to categorize and put into context. Luke, as he reviews the life of Christ in chronological order, returns to points of emphasis each time specific lessons come up again, and tries to highlight again those lessons and actions that embody Jesus the Chris. A few of those recurrent concepts are as follows:

1. Jesus Christ is the perfect Savior. Luke describes in detail how Jesus enters

into human history (Luke 1:5 - 4:13),
was predicted to do so (Luke 4:17-21),
and then how, through his sinlessness,
he provides himself as a perfect
sacrifice for our sins so that we may
be saved (Luke 5:20-26).

2. Jesus is a historically verifiable. Luke
   makes more emphasis on specific
   dates connecting Jesus to events and
   people in history than the other
   Gospels (Luke 2:1-2; 3:1,19, 21-22;
   23:2, 7-12).

3. Jesus cared deeply about people. Luke
   shares great detail about both how
   people felt about Jesus and how he
   felt about them. Luke gives the
   clearest picture of Jesus' authority
   (Luke 7:1-10), and the clearest picture
   of what it means to be a disciple of his
   (Luke 9:18-62).

4. Jesus had compassion. As a human,
   Jesus showed great sympathy toward
   those who were sick, poor, disliked, or
   sinful. He rejected no one who would
   believe in him (Luke 4:38-44).

5. Jesus has a close relationship with the
   Holy Spirit. The Holy Spirit was
   present at Jesus' birth (Luke 1:41ff),

baptism (Luke 3:21-22), temptation (Luke 4:1ff), ministry (Luke 4:18ff), and resurrection (Luke 24:36-53). The Holy Spirit plays a prominent role beyond the major events of Jesus' life, and Luke continues to emphasize the Spirit's importance throughout Acts (Luke 1:35; 10:21; 12:12; 11:13; Acts 2:1-4; 4:31).

6. Joy (Luke 8:13; 10:17; 21; Acts 8:8; 13:52)

7. Spiritual Songs and praise (Luke 2:13; 30; 18:43; 24:53; Acts 2:47; 3:8-9)

8. Luke emphasizes prayer (Luke 3:21; 6:12; 11:1-4; Acts 13:2; 4:24), and Jesus' reliance on prayer given significant place in His life (Luke 5:16; 6:12; 9:28-29; 11:1-13; 18:1-14; 22:32, 44; 23:46).

9. Luke establishes that Christ's plan included extending evangelism to all people (Luke 1:3; 2:20; 9:51-56; 19:9-10), which is another theme that runs uninterrupted into the Acts of the Apostles (Acts 9:15; 22:21 and 26:17).

10. Graciousness (Luke 6:20-25; 5:12-14; 7:11-16; 5:17-26; 18:15-17)

11. Christ as our Savior and Redeemer
    (Luke 2:11,38; 3:6; Acts 4:12; 2:36)

Outline:

A. Gospel Preface (1:1-4)

B. Birth and Preparation of Jesus, the
    Savior (1:5 - 4:13)

    1. The Savior's forerunner (1:5-80)

    2. Birth and Childhood of the Savior
    (2:1-52)

    3. The Savior's way prepared by the
    forerunner (3:1-20)

    4. Baptism, genealogy, and
    temptation of the Savior (3:21 -
    4:13)

C. The ministry of Jesus, the Savior (4:14
    - 21:38)

    1. The Galilean Ministry (4:14 - 9:50)

        a. The Savior's declaration of
        divine authority
        (4:14 - 5:32)

        b. The Savior begins a new order
        (5:33 - 6:49)

        c. The Savior reveals his power,
        authority, and
        glory (7:1 - 9:50)

2. The Ministry on the way to
    Jerusalem (9:51 -
    19:44)

    a. The Savior's mission,
        instructions, and
        warnings (9:51 -
        14:35)

    b. The Savior of the Lost (15:1-
        32)

    c. The Savior's commands to his
        followers (16:1 - 17:10)

    d. The Savior's end is near (17:11
        - 19:44)

3. Ministry in Jerusalem (19:45 -
    23:56)

    a. Silencing his enemies (19:45 -
        21:4)

    b. Coming destruction and death
        announced (21:5 - 22:6)

    c. Institution of the New
        Covenant (22:7-38)

    d. The Savior's death (22:39 -
        23:56)

D. Resurrection and Appearances of Jesus,
the Savior (24:1-53)

1. The Savior's triumph over death
(24:1-35)

2. Doubts of His followers dispelled
(24:36-49)

3. The Savior's return to the Father
(24:50-53)

The Apostle Matthew

"Follow Me." Matthew's call to Apostleship was that
simple. "Follow Me." Two little words, spoken by the
Christ, that would change the life of Matthew
immediately, and shape the lives of everyone to come
afterwards. "Follow Me." Those are the only words
Matthew chooses to record. Matthew simply rose and
followed Him. (Matt 9:9)

I don't know if Matthew intended a clear parallel between
his calling and the calling of Abraham. I am sure that
God intended us to see the simple similarity. God showed
His power to the world in the Creation (Genesis 1), the
Flood (Genesis 6), and at Babel (Genesis 11). When He
called Abraham into service, Abraham uprooted his
family and went without question or hesitation (Genesis
12). In much the same way, we know that Jesus had
already shown His deity. He had at least turned water to
wine (John 2), been confirmed as the Son of God at His
baptism (Luke 3:22), healed Peter's Mother-in-law, healed
great multitudes, cast out demons (Luke 4:38-42),
performed the miraculous catch of fish (Luke 5:3-10), and
healed both a leper and a paralytic (Luke 5:12-26).
Matthew likewise, when called into service, left everything
behind and followed Jesus (Luke 5:26-27).

Matthew was a man of means being a tax collector (Matt 9:9). Tax collectors, also called Publicans because of their employment in public office, were often disliked; as agents of the occupying state of Rome, they were hated as traitors. As agents of the government they were seen as self-serving opportunists, more focused on personal gain than national pride. A Jew could easily see them as turncoats, working in the service of the Roman government that oppressed Jewish self-rule.

What was Matthew like as a person? Why did he choose to be a tax collector? Both are tough questions with precious little guidance in Scripture to provide.

We know that Matthew threw a reception in Jesus' honor at once following his call (Matt 9:10). Luke makes it clear that the reception was at Matthew's own house, and that he had invited more tax-collectors and many others to attend (Luke 5:29). The house was filled with many sinners, and the scribes and Pharisees took note (Mark 2:15-16). It was in response to their accusations that Jesus states His personal purpose on earth by equating Himself to a physician; just as the sick need a doctor, Jesus came to call sinners (Mark 2:17). Do we realize that when Matthew records this statement, he is recording a statement about himself as a sinner? He goes further, reminding the learned Pharisees what is written in the prophets, that God desires compassion (Hosea 6:6).

Jesus' parable of the Publican and the Pharisee powerfully express this same sentiment (Luke 18:9-17). While conventional wisdom would say the Publican was more sinful than the Pharisee, it becomes clear that sinfulness is sinfulness. It is upon the penance of the heart, and humility in desire to approach God, that righteousness is achieved. In the parable the Publican shamelessly bares himself before God and anyone looking on. How much like this is Matthew? He invites many other sinful men to see him begin his journey with Jesus and does so in plain view of the Pharisees. Matthew certainly shares the exaltation of humility promised in the parable.

Likewise, let us consider the story of Zacchaeus. Only Luke records this familiar story from our childhood (Luke 19:1-10). In it, Zacchaeus was a chief tax collector. He also wanted to see Jesus, then, much to his surprise, Jesus called him into service. Zacchaeus found himself welcoming Christ into his home (Luke 19:5) and was glad to share his prosperity with Him (Luke 19:6). He made amends for any wrongs he had committed and helped the poor with his wealth (Luke 19:8).

Why would we consider the story of Zacchaeus, a different tax-collector not even recorded by Matthew? Think about this. Zacchaeus hosted Jesus in his home, as we just noted. Jesus clearly moved from Nazareth, making Capernaum near the Sea of Galilee His new home base early in his ministry (Matt 4:13-17). Matthew was also from Capernaum (Matt 9:1; Luke 4:31, 5:27). Is it so difficult for us to believe that Jesus may have depended on Matthew's support early in His ministry? Even if that were not necessary, it is clear from Matthew's reception of Christ that he would have been willing to do so.

Regarding Matthew's mundane statistics, we also know a few additional facts. As we studied, we know he was a tax collector (Matt 9:9), who lived in or near Capernaum (Mark 2:1-17). We also know that he was a son of Alphaeus (Mark 2:14), and was likely at least a half-brother to another Apostle, James the Son of Alphaeus (Mark 3:18).

He is referred to as Levi in some verses and Matthew in others. It appears Levi may have been his given or familial name. Matthew may have been his familiar name or a name given him by Jesus; in Hebrew, Matthew means "gift of God."

We know he was one of the 12 Apostles (Matt 10:2-4; Mark 3:16-19; Luke 6:14-16) and was granted the power to heal the sick and cast out demons as part of his commission to preach that the kingdom of heaven is at hand (Matt 10:5-8).

Matthew was present at the Last Supper (Matt 26:20), saw Jesus after His resurrection (John 20:19-25), and for the Great Commission (Matt 28:16-20). We also know that

Matthew was there to see his Lord ascend into heaven (Acts 1:8).

So, what shall we say of Matthew? He was clearly part of the sinfulness of the world before Jesus called him, being a publican and having many other publicans as friends. He understood the weight of his calling, leaving that prosperous vocation in favor of the hardships of Apostleship. He showed generosity in hosting a meal for Christ, and it is possible he helped finance Christ's early ministry. Matthew was a trusted disciple who remained loyal to Jesus throughout his life, death, and continued to serve him afterward.

Somewhere in these experiences, he was stirred to begin writing down the things he heard Jesus say, emphasizing how those sayings and actions fulfilled the promises in the Mosaic law and the prophets. He went from service to Rome in occupying his homeland, to service for God liberating all men.

Choosing a verse to encapsulate Matthew, I easily choose:

> *"And He said to them, 'Follow Me, and I wil l make you fishers of men.'"*
> *(NASV: Matt 4:19)*

Traditional history is mixed on what came of Matthew after the Bible account leaves him. Some of the oldest documentation says he traveled to Persia, Macedonia,

Syria, Parthia, Media, and Ethiopia to minister to others in public service and those in leadership roles in their governments. Some older stories suggest Matthew eventually met a martyr's death for his outspokenness for Christ.

In any case, the principal thing we can say of Matthew the man is that when he heard those fateful words, "Follow Me," he went.

The Gospel of Matthew

What:

The Gospel According to Matthew.

Why:

Jesus, the fulfillment of the Law and Prophets

When:

AD 58 or 59.

Many scholars place the date of this writing a little later near AD 70, and some evidence could support an extremely late writing shortly after AD 90. Dating this book is exceedingly difficult, but a date near the earliest possible dates appears to be most consistent with facts about judgment and resurrection relied upon by Paul in his earlier letters.

Where:

Antioch in Syria. While this location is traditionally attributed, it is consistent with unique Greek words used to reference coinage (Matt 17:24, 27).

From Who:

Matthew the Apostle and Tax Collector.

To Whom:

Jewish Christians and those who seek to understand that Jesus' mission was the culmination of God's work with man, resulting in spreading hope to all nations (Matt 28:16-20).

Setting:

The Roman Empire under Nero (54 to 68 AD). The empire had a universal language and an excellent road system. The Jewish dispersion had begun, and Matthew was seeking to provide hope and guidance in those difficult times.

Key Verse:

> *"Do not think that I came to abolish the Law or the Prophets; I did not come to abolish, but to fulfill."*
>
> *(NASV: Matt 5:17)*

Distinguishing Characteristics:

Matthew does not suppose to put his account into clear chronological order. A cursory comparison of Luke's account, which is known to be in order (Luke 1:1-4), allows us to see that Matthew goes only very roughly in chronological order. In fact, Matthew only presents three main things in order in his account: Jesus' Birth & Childhood come first, Jesus' Death & Resurrection come last, and everything else comes in between. In that 'in between' section, most scholars I am aware of see that Matthew divided Jesus' teaching into five topical sections.

Understanding this concept, this would be the simplest outline of Matthew's Gospel:

1) Introduction: Jesus is of the Right Bloodline
   (Matt 1:1 – 4:25)

   This section specifically shows Jesus' rightful place as leader and teacher to Israel by spelling out His royal genealogy and foretells His place as King to all by pointedly including the Gentiles in Jesus' heritage (Tamar, Rahab, Ruth, Hittite). His Deity and Royalty is emphasized throughout the birth account (1:18-23). This section culminates with the Divine proclamation "This is my beloved Son." (3:17). Matthew again foretells the coming great commission by recording in this section that Jesus' begins His ministry outside Judea (4:5).

2) Lesson 1: Jesus is the Teacher of New Commands
   (Matt 5:1 – 7:29)

This section is commonly referred to as 'the Sermon on the Mount', and is characterized by Jesus exercising His authority to supersede the Mosaic Law (5:19, 22, 28, 32, 39, 44) and to teach His disciples what to say when He sent them out (7:28-29).

3) Lesson 2: Jesus is Sovereign God of the Universe (Matt 8:1 – 10:42)

Matthew chooses to record 10 consecutive miracles that establish Jesus' authority (Leper 8:2, Paralytic 8:5, Fever 8:14, Demons 8:16, Stills Sea 8:23, Demoniac in Tombs 8:28, Paralytic 9:1, Dead Girl 9:18, Two Blind Men 9:27, Mute Demon-possessed 9:32). He establishes Jesus' authority to forgive sin by placing it in the context of this demonstration of Christ's sovereignty (9:8). Jesus then imbues His disciples with authority to work miracles (10:1), formally names the 12 Apostles (10:5), instructs them on how to act (10:16), and on the meaning of discipleship (10:24).

4) Lesson 3: Jesus The Expected Lord & Redeemer (Matt 11:1 – 13:52)

John the Baptizer's question: Jesus is "The Expected One" (11:3, Psalm 118:26). He honors John (11:7), chastises unbelievers (11:20), rules the Sabbath (12:1, Isaiah 42:1), promises salvation to the Gentiles (12:18, Isaiah 42:1), heals a blind-dumb demon-possessed man (12:22), and reprimands the Pharisees (12:25).

He closes with parables about evangelism (13:1), how to interpret them (13:10), and more evangelistic parables (13:24).

5) Lesson 4: Jesus is Rabbi to the Gentiles too
   (Matt 13:53 – 18:35)

   Matthew makes plain in this section that Jesus came for all peoples, not solely Jews, as he shows the crowds at the Synagogue in Nazareth were astonished (13:54), but Jews resisted (13:57). Jesus' disciples accepted (14:33), so did the Gentile woman (15:22). Out-teaches Pharisees (16:1), Peter's confession (16:21), Jesus Transfigured (17:1) and makes new application of known Jewish teachings (18:1), focusing on genuine and open forgiveness (18:21).

6) Lesson 5: Jesus is King
   (19:1 – 25:46)

   Jesus enters Jerusalem as a King (21:1), cleanses the Temple as King of Kings (21:10), and only answers questions about His authority (21:23) with parables of obedience (21:28), parables of judgment (21:33), parables of true citizenship (22:1), and teachings on priorities (22:15), resurrection (22:23), and the greatest command (22:34). He exposes the false rulers of the day (23:1) and teaches His closest followers about His Judgment (24:1ff and 25:1ff).

7) Closing: Jesus is the Sacrificial King
(Matt 26:1 – 28:30)

Jesus dies with self-control unseen among men. In
this death, a Gentile sums up His life best: "Truly this
was the Son of God" (27:54).

In this topical approach to Jesus' life and teachings,
Matthew couches everything in Judaic thought and
emphasizes the authority Jesus has as Christ because He
is the fulfillment of the promise, using the term "fulfill"
more than any other Bible book (1:22; 2:15, 17, 23; 4:14;
8:17; 12:17; 13:35; 21:4; 26:56; 27:9). Matthew makes the
most reference to Old Testament scripture of the
Gospels (At least 53 direct quotes, 76 other or partial
references; see the table of Old Testament citations and
allusions found in Matthew for examples.).

Matthew refers to Jesus as the "Son of David", a Jewish
Old Testament term at least 8 times, more than all the
other Gospels combined (1:1; 9:27; 12:23; 15:22; 20:30,
31; 21:9, 15). Similarly, he calls Him by "Son of God" at
least 23 times; "This is My Son" twice (3:17, 17:5), and
"Son of Man" at least 31 times. (See table of Old
Testament citations and allusions found in Matthew for
examples.)

Put in the simplest terms I can come up with, Matthew is
the statement that 1) God through Christ did something
completely new with this Testament, and at the same time

2) we cannot do away with, but rather must embrace our heritage in, the Old Law because Jesus is the fulfillment of it (5:17-19, 21-22, 27-28, 31-32, 33, 38-39, 43-44).

The Apostle John

The Apostle John

John, known by many names throughout scripture—Son of Zebedee, Boanerges (Son of Thunder), The Beloved Disciple, The Evangelist, The Revealer—presents the most dramatic transformation of any Gospel writer. Born to Zebedee (Matt 4:21) and Salome (Matt 27:56; Mark 16:1) somewhere near Nazareth in Galilee, John spent his early years working alongside his father and brother James as fishermen on the Sea of Galilee (Matt 4:18-22). Though the exact location of his birth remains uncertain, he likely lived near Cana or in Capernaum, where his fishing business operated in partnership with Peter and his brother Andrew (Luke 5:10).

John's personality emerges vividly through the Gospel accounts, revealing a man of intense passions and contradictions. He could be rancorous and blustery (Luke 9:54), as when he and his brother wanted to call down fire from heaven upon an inhospitable Samaritan village. This incident earned them both the nickname "Sons of Thunder" from Jesus himself (Mark 3:17). His condemnatory nature (Mark 9:38) showed itself when he tried to stop someone from driving out demons in Jesus' name simply because the man wasn't part of their immediate circle. The self-centeredness of his early discipleship (Mark 10:35-37) became most apparent when he and James, through their mother, requested the positions at Jesus' right and left hand in the kingdom (Mark 10:35-43)—a request that revealed their fundamental misunderstanding of the nature of Christ's kingdom.

Yet this same fierce intensity that made John quick to judgment and eager for position would be transformed into something beautiful. The passionate fire that once sought to destroy a village (Luke 9:54-55) would become a burning love that would sustain the church through persecution. The boldness that once demanded special privilege would become the courage to stand at the foot of the cross when others fled. His passionate nature, evident in both his bold statements before authorities (Acts 4:13) and his profound expressions of love throughout his epistles (1 John 4), became the very quality that enabled him to grasp and communicate the depths of divine love. As Acts records, even the religious leaders recognized something extraordinary in this "unschooled" fisherman—they saw he had been with Jesus.

John occupied a unique position among the Twelve. He was among the first four apostles called to be "fishers of men" (Matt 4:19) and quickly became part of the intimate "inner three" along with Peter and his brother James (Mark 5:37; 9:2; 13:3; 14:33). These three witnessed moments others did not: the raising of Jairus' daughter, the glory of the Transfiguration (Mark 9:2-8), and the agony in Gethsemane (Matt 26:36-46). But even within this inner circle, John held a special place. At the Last Supper, which he had been sent to prepare (Luke 22:8), he reclined next to Jesus in the position of honor (John 13:23), close enough to lean against the Master's chest. It was John whom Jesus entrusted with the care of His mother Mary as He hung dying on the cross (John 19:26-27)—a responsibility that speaks volumes about both Jesus' trust in John and John's transformation from a "Son of Thunder" to a son Mary could depend upon.

The tradition suggests that John was married, although Scripture provides no details about his family life. What we do know is that his household became integral to the foundation of the early church. After the resurrection, John emerged as one of the key leaders, possibly even an Elder, of the Jerusalem church (Galatians 2:9, Acts 15). Paul himself recognized John as one of the "pillars" of the church alongside Peter and James, the brother of Jesus. Together with Peter, John healed the lame man at the temple gate and boldly proclaimed the gospel before the Sanhedrin (Acts 3-4:8), the same body that had condemned Jesus. Their fearless preaching and miraculous healings continued until persecution eventually drove John to exile on the island of Patmos (Rev 1:1, 9), where isolation became the setting for the greatest revelation ever given to humanity.

John's literary legacy stands unique among the Gospel writers. His contributions include not only the Gospel of John but also the Epistles of 1st, 2nd and 3rd John, and the book of Revelation—a body of work that spans from the most intimate portrait of Jesus' earthly ministry to the cosmic vision of Christ's ultimate triumph. Writing from the perspective of advanced age, with decades to reflect on what he had witnessed, John presents a Jesus who is simultaneously the eternal Word who was with God in the beginning and the friend who wept at Lazarus' tomb. His is the Gospel that records Jesus' most profound theological discourses while also preserving the most tender human moments.

The life lesson that emerges from John's journey is profound in its simplicity: love overcomes all challenges. The young man who wanted to destroy those who rejected Jesus became the aged apostle who could write nothing more profound than "Little children, love one another." The disciple who sought position and power became the one who understood that God is love, and that this love, demonstrated in Christ's sacrifice, must be the defining characteristic of all who follow Him. His transformation from a "Son of Thunder" to "The Apostle of Love" proves the power of prolonged exposure to Jesus' presence and teaching.

Those seeking to see the face of God and understand His love for humanity will find it in John's writings. His theology is complex and compelling, presenting Jesus as both fully divine and deeply personal. Through John's eyes, we see a Savior who is the Creator of the universe yet calls us friends, who holds all power yet washes His disciples' feet, who is the source of eternal life yet shares in our human experiences. John is not a polished theology professor but somewhat resembles a village elder—one who has lived long enough to see beyond the surface of things, to understand that the greatest mysteries are often the simplest truths, and that the most profound theology can be summarized in the declaration that God so loved the world.

Personal Interactions with Jesus

John's relationship with Jesus started with a simple call. He was among the first four men Jesus asked to become "fishers of men" (Matt 4:19). John dropped his fishing nets immediately. Something about Jesus made him leave everything behind without a second thought.

Jesus saw something special in John and his brother James. He nicknamed them "Boanerges"—Sons of Thunder (Mark 3:17). The name fit. These brothers had fiery tempers and big personalities. But Jesus saw more than just their rough edges. He saw what they could become.

Jesus chose John for His inner circle, along with Peter and James (Mark 5:37; 9:2; 13:3; 14:33). These three got to see things the other disciples missed. On the mountain, John watched Jesus transform before his eyes (Mark 9:2-8). Christ's face shone like the sun. His clothes became dazzling white. Moses and Elijah appeared and talked with Jesus. John fell to the ground, terrified and amazed.

Later, in Gethsemane's garden, Jesus brought John along for His hardest night (Matt 26:36-46). While John struggled to stay awake, he saw Jesus in agony. He watched his Master pray desperately about the suffering to come. These moments—both glorious and painful—showed John who Jesus really was.

But being close to Jesus also meant getting corrected by Him. When John bragged about stopping someone from casting out demons in Jesus' name (Mark 9:38), Jesus told him not to. God's work was bigger than their little group. When John and James wanted to destroy a Samaritan village with fire from heaven (Luke 9:54-55), Jesus rebuked them sharply. They did not understand His mission yet.

The brothers' ambition showed most clearly when their mother asked Jesus for a favor. She wanted her sons sitting at His right and left hand in the kingdom (Mark 10:35-43). Jesus asked them a hard question: "Can you drink the cup I'm going to drink?" They said yes, not knowing He meant suffering and death. Jesus used this moment to teach them about servant leadership. Greatness meant serving others, not ruling over them.

Jesus trusted John with important tasks. He sent John and Peter to prepare the upper room for the Last Supper (Luke 22:8). At that final meal, John sat right next to Jesus in the place of honor (John 13:23). He was close enough to lean against Jesus' chest, close enough to hear His heartbeat. This was not just about seating arrangements. It showed their deep friendship.

At the cross, most disciples ran away in fear. John stayed. He stood with the women, watching Jesus die. From the cross, Jesus gave John a sacred responsibility—to care for His mother Mary (John 19:26). Think about that. In His dying moments, Jesus entrusted His mother to John. That is the ultimate sign of trust and love.

After the resurrection, John's special connection with Jesus continued. When Mary Magdalene said the tomb was empty, John raced Peter there (John 20:3, 4). He arrived first but waited for Peter to enter. When John finally looked inside and saw the grave clothes, he understood. Jesus was alive. John would later write extensively about this moment of seeing and believing (John 20:5-8). It became central to his message.

Days later, the disciples went fishing. They caught nothing all night. At dawn, a stranger on the shore told them to cast their nets on the other side. The nets filled with fish—the same miracle Jesus had performed when He first called them (John 21:2-7). John recognized Him instantly. "It's the Lord!" he shouted to Peter. While others wondered, John knew. He always recognizes Jesus first.

John outlived all the other apostles. Reliable accounts from the second century say he was released from exile on Patmos and returned to Ephesus. He died there around 100 A.D., probably from old age. He was the only apostle to die naturally.

> *"So when Jesus saw His mother, and the disciple whom He loved standing nearby, He *said to His mother, "Woman, behold, your son!"*
>
> *(NASV: John 19:26)*

Some stories about John's death are less certain. One says he died on Patmos in 96 A.D. Another claims he was executed by being lowered into boiling oil in 99 A.D. Some even say God took him to heaven alive in 100 A.D. But the most believable tradition is simple: John lived longest, had the most time to think about what he had seen, and spent his final years telling everyone about the Jesus he knew so well—the Jesus who was his teacher, his Lord, and his dearest friend.

The Gospel of John

What:

The Gospel According to John.

Why:

Jesus, Lord and Creator. Emphasize the 'why' we would follow Jesus: he performed signs, not for the purpose of proving His deity, but to help us in our unbelief (John 20:30-31). He is not only the Almighty Creator of the Universe (John 1:3), but also a warm and kindhearted friend (John 3:29; 11:11; 15:12-13).

When:

Between AD 85 and AD 90

Most scholars agree with a late date for the writing of the Gospel According to John, near the end of the first century. A few responsible historians do place the writing as early as AD 70, just before the destruction of Jerusalem, but the weight of evidence puts the writing after the Temple is destroyed.

Where:

Ephesus.

From Who:

John the Apostle. He was the brother of James and son of Zebedee (Matt 4:21-22; Mark 1:19-20), business partner to Simon Peter (Luke 5:10), and among the three Apostles in the 'inner circle' (Mark 5:37; 9:2; 14:32-33). Some argue that this Gospel was written by the Elder of Ephesus named John, but the deep affection expressed between the author and Jesus strongly suggests it was authored by John the beloved Apostle (John 13:23). If John, the Elder of Ephesus, was involved it is only historically supportable and consistent literarily in the role of scribe.

To Whom:

New Christians and those who would be Christians who want to know the person of Jesus and the manifestation of his Deity.

Setting:

The Roman Empire under Domitian
Caesar (81 – 96 AD). In a world in which
the Jewish nation is no more, after the
destruction of Jerusalem, before John is
exiled to Patmos. Most of the first-hand
witnesses to Christ have died and the first
generation of Church leadership who did
not know Christ physically are guiding the
body of believers.

Key Verse:

> *"Many other signs therefore Jesus also
> performed in the presence of the disciples,
> which are not written in this book; but these
> have been written that you may believe that
> Jesus is the Christ, the Son of God; and that
> believing you may have life in His name."*
> *(NASV; John 20:30-31)*

Distinguishing Characteristics:

John, despite his warm family approach and low-educated
writing style, carries among the most complicated
metaphor architectures in all literature. John sets up and
maintains "4 images" as the vehicle for every exchange:
birth, water, light, and sight. The concepts of birth and
water are so intertwined as to be inseparable, then those

appear in context with wine, blood, cleansing and thirst. These first two images of birth and water appear 47 times and 53 times, respectively. Similarly, John ties the concepts of light and sight, which appear 68 times and 168 times, to one another and uses them as an allegory of salvation.

Sometimes called the "reasoning" gospel as it takes great effort to explain not only how to follow Jesus, but WHY we would want to (1:14). His main vehicle for this is giving us insight into the person of Jesus whom the disciples saw daily and allows us insight as they interact with Him. He spends his greatest energies on time Jesus spent with his disciples in and around their hometown in casual settings, and records some of Jesus' 1-on-1 conversations.

Matthew and Mark record primarily the Judean ministry, with Luke adding the Perean. John spends little time on these ministries and instead focuses on the Galilean ministry. Ironically, the other three Gospels make it appear as though Jesus only appears in Jerusalem a week before His death, but John makes it clear that He made at least four separate trips there during his ministry (John 2:13; 5:1; 7:10; 12:12).

Mark begins his Gospel with an adult Jesus, Matthew begins with a lineage reaching Abraham and records some details of Jesus youth, Luke begins with a lineage reaching

Adam and records many details of Jesus' birth. John begins with Jesus before time began, and the only lineage recorded is the one He shares with the Father in the Creation (John 1:1-4, 14).

In stark contrast to the other Gospels, John records none of Jesus' parables, no miracles involving lepers, and demons are never mentioned, much less cast out. Instead, John chooses to record a smaller number of miracles and include those that took place on the Sabbath, involved sight, or gave Jesus other opportunity to demonstrate that He is not only Lord and Creator, but establisher and completer of the Mosaic Law who is equal to the Father (John 5:6-19 and similar).

John never records the names of the 12 Apostles and does not mention the Bread and the Wine at the Last Supper, choosing instead to record that Jesus washed the Apostle's feet (John 13:1-5). While Mark focuses more on the servant heart of Christ, John does call it to mind in cases like these to show that Jesus is not only sovereign, but humble. It is this very seeming paradox that motivates much of John's writing.

Records Jesus' longest discourses; simply 'sits and listens.' (2nd half of Chapter 5, 2nd half of Chapter 6, 1st half of Chapter 10, end of Chapter 12, all of Chapters 14-17, and many other 5-10 verse blocks).

John records many stories, discussions, and interactions that the other Gospels do not, including: Jesus discussion with Nicodemus (John 3), the Samaritan Woman at the Well (John 4), Healing the Man Born Blind (John 9), Raising Lazarus from the Dead (John 11), and Jesus' Prayer for His Disciples (John 17), as examples. Where John varies from the Synoptic Gospels it is, again, always for the purpose of showing the inextricable tie between Jesus' humanity and His deity.

John cites "three sevens", "four images", coming in 'my name', signs, witness and testify, obeying 'he who sent me', 'keep my commandments', with time we 'now understand' what He said, and creates this work that could be outlined in any of 13 different primary ways in a framework of enduring and all-powerful love. John clearly believed that in knowing Christ, we can know we are saved and believed that knowledge of the written and living Word of God is an assurance to us. He used the term 'know' at least 77 times, and it is clear he wanted to assure us that what we believe is certain.

Rather than close the study of this Gospel with an effort at an outline that will certainly fall short, I have decided instead to close with a couple of tables. First is the table of the 'Three Sevens,' listing the seven miracles Jesus worked during His ministry, His seven sermons recorded by John, and the seven statements Jesus made regarding "I AM." Second is a series of lists showing in what verses each of the four images may be found: birth 47 times, water 53 times, light 68 times and sight 168 times.

The "Three Sevens" in John's Gospel

Seven Signs	Seven Sermons	Seven "I AM" Sayings
Water to Wine 2:1-11	New Birth 3:1-21	The Bread of Life 6:35, 41, 48, 51
Nobleman's Son 4:46-54	Water of Life 4:41-42	The Light of the World 8:12
Paralyzed Man 5:5-18	Equal with the Father 5:19-47	The Door 10:2, 7, 9
Feeding the Five Thousand 6:1-15	Bread of Life 6:22-66	The Good Shepherd 10:11-14
Walks on Water 6:16-21	From the Father 7:1-52	The Resurrection and the Life 11:25
Heals the Blind 9:1-7	The Light of the World 8:12-59	The Way, the Truth, the Life 14:6
Lazarus Raised 11:1-14	The Good Shepherd 10:1-21	The Vine 15:1, 5

Four Images:

Birth – 47 times: Concepts from the Greek genna, meaning "descent, birth, or origination". The closest wording, and those chosen for this study are: gennao, birth, to beget, to bring forth; ginomai, to come into being. 1:3, 1:3, 1:3, 1:6, 1:10, 1:12, 1:13, 2:9, 3:3, 3:4, 3:4, 3:5, 3:6, 3:6, 3:7, 3:8, 3:25, 4:14, 5:4, 5:9, 5:14, 6:16, 6:17, 7:43, 8:33, 8:41, 8:58, 9:1, 9:2, 9:19, 9:20, 9:27, 9:32, 9:34, 9:39, 10:16, 10:19, 10:22, 10:35, 12:30, 12:36, 13:21, 14:22, 16:21, 16:21, 18:37, 19:36

Water – 53 times: Water, waters, pool, sea, spat, well, clay, bathed, wash, basin: 1:26, 1:31, 1:33, 2:6, 2:7, 2:9, 2:9, 3:5, 3:23, 4:6, 4:6, 4:7, 4:10, 4:11, 4:12, 4:13, 4:14, 4:14, 4:14, 4:14, 4:15, 4:46, 5:2, 5:3, 5:4, 5:4, 5:7, 6:1, 6:16, 6:17, 6:18, 6:19, 6:22, 6:25, 7:38, 9:6, 9:6, 9:6, 9:7, 9:11, 9:11, 9:14, 9:15, 13:5, 13:5, 13:6, 13:8, 13:8, 13:10, 13:14, 19:34, 21:1, 21:7

Light – 68 times: Light, dark, night, day, evening, morning, bright, dazzle: 1:4, 1:5, 1:5, 1:7, 1:8, 1:8, 1:9, 1:29, 1:35, 1:39, 1:43, 2:1, 3:19, 3:19, 3:20, 3:20, 3:21, 5:9, 5:35, 6:16, 6:17, 6:22, 6:39, 6:40, 6:44, 6:54, 7:37, 8:2, 8:12, 8:12, 8:12, 8:56, 9:4, 9:4, 9:5, 9:14, 11:9, 11:9, 11:9, 11:10, 11:10, 11:24, 11:53, 12:7, 12:12, 12:35, 12:35, 12:35, 12:35, 12:36, 12:36, 12:36, 12:36, 12:46, 12:46, 12:48, 13:30, 14:20, 16:23, 16:26, 19:14, 19:31, 19:39, 19:42, 20:1, 20:19, 21:3, 21:4

Sight – 168 times: Blind, sight, see, eye(s), witness, testimony, perceive, look, window, mirror, glass: 1:7, 1:7, 1:8, 1:15, 1:18, 1:19, 1:29, 1:32, 1:33, 1:34, 1:34, 1:36, 1:39, 1:39, 1:42, 1:46, 1:47, 1:48, 1:50, 1:50, 1:51, 2:18, 2:25, 3:3, 3:11, 3:11, 3:26, 3:28, 3:32, 3:32, 3:32, 3:33, 3:36, 4:19, 4:29, 4:35, 4:35, 4:45, 4:48, 4:54, 5:3, 5:6, 5:20, 5:31, 5:31, 5:32, 5:32, 5:33, 5:34, 5:36, 5:37, 5:37, 5:39, 6:5, 6:14, 6:22, 6:24, 6:26, 6:30, 6:36, 6:46, 6:46, 7:4, 7:7, 7:26, 7:52, 8:13, 8:13, 8:14, 8:14, 8:17, 8:18, 8:18, 8:38, 8:51, 8:56, 8:56, 8:57, 9:1, 9:2, 9:6, 9:8, 9:10, 9:11, 9:11, 9:13, 9:14, 9:15, 9:15, 9:17, 9:17, 9:18, 9:18, 9:18, 9:19, 9:19, 9:20, 9:21, 9:24, 9:25, 9:25, 9:26, 9:30, 9:32, 9:37, 9:39, 9:39, 9:40, 9:41, 9:41, 10:21, 10:25, 10:41, 11:31, 11:32, 11:33, 11:34, 11:37, 11:40, 11:41, 12:9, 12:17, 12:18, 12:19, 12:19, 12:21, 12:40, 12:40, 12:40, 12:41, 13:22, 14:7, 14:8, 14:9, 14:9, 15:24, 15:26, 15:27, 16:16, 16:17, 16:19, 16:22, 17:1, 18:23, 18:26, 18:37, 19:6, 19:26, 19:33, 19:35, 19:35, 19:37, 20:1, 20:5, 20:5, 20:8, 20:11, 20:18, 20:20, 20:25, 20:25, 20:27, 20:29, 20:29, 21:9, 21:20, 21:24, 21:24

The 'four images' are intermixed 52 times in Chapter 9 – in 41 verses. We can take away the distinct impression that birth into our new life is something born of water, we see our way to it with the light of Jesus' life, and we illuminate our lives with the light of our salvation thereafter. 9:1, 9:1, 9:2, 9:2, 9:4, 9:4, 9:5, 9:6, 9:6, 9:6, 9:6, 9:7, 9:8, 9:10, 9:11, 9:11, 9:11, 9:11, 9:13, 9:14, 9:14, 9:14, 9:15, 9:15, 9:15, 9:17, 9:17, 9:18, 9:18, 9:18, 9:19, 9:19, 9:19, 9:20, 9:20, 9:21, 9:24, 9:25, 9:25, 9:26, 9:27, 9:30, 9:32, 9:32, 9:34, 9:37, 9:39, 9:39, 9:39, 9:40, 9:41, 9:41

Select Study: Christ's Birth

Some who read the Gospel accounts quickly become frustrated when they try to read the first-hand account of a story, only to find that they cannot find the story as they remember it. The account of Christ's birth is no exception. The commercialization of Jesus' birth has provided us with vivid Technicolor composites of the account. Many of those, unfortunately, also make several additions and embellishments to that event.

A simple list of what scriptures to read, in what order, to paint a full picture of the birth is straightforward to assemble. I have also tried to add some notes about the amount of time that passes between each passage of scripture. Where that passage of time is confirmable by scripture it is simply said. Where the passing of time is either traditional or only supportable by extra-Biblical texts, I have called those out.

Here is the account of the birth as given us by inspired scripture:

Approximately 6 B.C. (traditional) at the Temple in Jerusalem, the Angel Gabriel Announces the Herald John and the coming Christ to Zechariah.

Luke 1:5-25

Six months later, in Nazareth, an Angel tells Mary that she will bear the Christ.

Luke 1:26-38

Right away, Mary travels to Judah to visit Elizabeth.

Luke 1:39-56

Three months later, John the Baptizer is Born in the hill country in Judea.

Luke 1:57-79

At some time shortly after Mary returns to Nazareth from Judea, she is found to be with child. She is at least 3 months pregnant when she returns. The Angel tells Joseph that Mary will have a Child conceived of the Holy Spirit.

Matthew 1:18-25a

Jesus is Born in Bethlehem. This is certainly 15+ months after Zechariah was first told of the coming Christ and is summer to fall 5 B.C. (historical / traditional).

Luke 2:1-7, John 1:14a

Angels proclaim Jesus' birth to the shepherds, near Bethlehem, while Joseph, Mary and Jesus are still in the stables.

Luke 2:8-20

Eight days later, Jesus named and circumcised. This took place at a synagogue near Bethlehem.

Matthew 1:25b, Luke 2:21

Forty days later, Jesus is presented to the priests at the Temple in Jerusalem. (Jesus is now certainly 48 days old.)

Luke 2:22-39a

Some time between 48 days and 1 year after birth the Magi from the East visit Jesus to worship Him. It is possible this took place in Bethlehem but is far more likely it took place in Nazareth (uncertain).

Matthew 2:1-12

An Angel warns Joseph that Herod plans to kill the newborn boys. Joseph, Mary, and Jesus flee to Egypt. Jesus at this time is certainly at least 48 days old and is likely to be between 1 and 2 years of age.

Matthew 2:13-18

An Angel of the Lord tells Joseph that Herod is dead.
Joseph, Mary, and Jesus' return to Nazareth. This is likely
to happen when Jesus is over 2 years old, in late 4 B.C. or
early 3 B.C. (historical).

Matthew 2:19-23

Select Study: Baptism

Treatise on baptism.

Jesus tells Nicodemus that unless he is born again, of water and the spirit, he cannot see the kingdom of heaven (John 3:3, 5). What birth and what water is this?

Paul already told us that to be in Christ means to walk a new life (2 Cor 5:17) and that new life begins at baptism (Romans 6:2-4).

John hearkens all the way back to a Covenant God made with Israel (Ezekiel 36:25ff), promising to make them spiritually clean after they are washed with water. He echoes this sentiment strongly when Jesus washes the disciples' feet, saying unless Jesus washes them with water, they have no part of him (John 13:8).

John records when Jesus insists, we put on an attitude of accepting his commands (John 15), hearkening back to Paul's words that we put Jesus on and become clothed in him at our baptism (Gal 3:27).

It is baptism that saves us (1 Pet 3:21) and that washes away our sins (Acts 22:16).

Select Study: Jewish Calendar & The Year of Jesus' Passion

The Jewish Calendar

The Jewish day accounting and calendar differ from our modern calendar. It is easy to become confused or to make the comparison more complicated than it needs to be. I will be as clear as possible.

In our modern 'day' system, midnight is a defined point in time that will vary in its distance from sunset and sunrise. In the Jewish calendar, sunset always defines the moment when the day and date change.

Jews view sunset as the 'end of the day'. This meant, to them, that all time that has taken place since the last sunset is 'today'. We often try to think of the day 'starting' after sunset, but every authoritative book written by a Jew I have found refers to sunset as the 'end of the day'; we may discover adopting that thinking helpful.

The Jewish week begins on Sunday. Sunday has been the first day of the week since the earliest verifiable calendars.

Our modern calendar is a fixed solar calendar, maintained by defining a point on Earth as the 'start of rotation' and using it as the reference point for defining the year. We have the same 12 months that have been in use since the time of Caesar Augustus and are typically 30 or 31 days in length. A leap day is added to February once every 4 years, and has been since approximately 45 B.C., when Julius Caesar implemented the Julian calendar (the Gregorian Adjustment to drop Leap Day in certain century years was added in 1582). Our 'year' designation, theoretically, counts time since the birth of Christ. Most scholars agree that when our modern 'year' was first accounted in about 525 A.D. by Dionysius Exiguus, he miscalculated by 4 to 9 years. This is almost impossible to verify precisely, as the Julian and Gregorian calendars were not unified until much later. In the year 2025, most scholars would agree that Christ was actually born between 2029 and 2034 years ago.

The Jewish calendar counts years from the traditional date of Creation, which is set at 3761 B.C.E. According to this reckoning, the current year is 5786. This system—known as *Anno Mundi*—was not used in biblical times, where dates were typically recorded by regnal years or major events like the Exodus or the building of the Temple. Counting from Creation only became standard in Jewish communities during late antiquity.

Although the calendar is not fully verified by inspired scripture, it has been continuously maintained since around 1200 B.C., when historical records begin to align more reliably. Earlier dates in the Jewish calendar show discrepancies, but from roughly 900 B.C. onward, its accuracy improves—especially when cross-referenced with the Babylonian calendar, which was highly advanced in astronomical observation and intercalation methods. Though Julian accounting did not formally begin until 45 B.C., between 900 B.C. and 1258 A.D., the Jewish calendar is more consistent than the extended Julian calendar.

The Jewish Calendar is a lunisolar calendar, meaning that its primary measurement is by the month, and the start of the religious year always begins with the lunar cycle matching a season. It has 12 months, all typically with 29 or 30 days. As 'leap years' need to be added, a 13th month is included between months 11 and 12. Those months are:

Nisan (30 days)
Iyar (29 days)
Sivan (30 days)
Tammuz (29 days)
Av (30 days)
Elul (29 days)
Tishrei (30 days)
Cheshvan (29 or 30 days)

Kislev (29 or 30 days)

Tevet (29 days)

Shevat (30 days)

Adar I (30 days; only included in leap years, 7 out of 19
years)

Adar (29 days; called Adar II in leap years)

While Nisan is considered the first month for religious
purposes, the Jewish civil new year (Rosh Hashanah)
occurs on the 1st of Tishrei. For the religious calendar, to
determine the beginning of Nisan, the Hebrews would
calculate when the first new moon would appear,
ensuring that Passover (the 14th of Nisan) fell after the
vernal equinox. Repeating it in plain language, the Jewish
Priests would calculate the start of the year such that 14
Nisan was always the first Full Moon after the Vernal
Equinox.

Comparing with our modern calendar, the Vernal
Equinox always takes place around March 20th or 21st.
This means that the Jewish religious year's first month
(Nisan) typically falls between our modern March and
April, and always started the day of a New Moon.

The leap month is added every 2 or 3 years to account for
the lunar cycle being shorter than the solar year when
calculated monthly (365/12). That leap month was used
in conjunction with variable-length months (by adding
days to Cheshvan and Kislev), making the entire Jewish

calendar a repeating cycle of 235 months; there are 7 leap years out of every 19 years. This system is highly accurate, with an error of only 1 day every 231 years, compared to our modern fixed solar calendar.

The Jewish Passover was not celebrated on a fixed day of the week. Its celebration is always on the 14th day of Nisan. Passover is more than a single day, which can get confusing. Some sort of celebration continues for 7 days for Passover; Nisan 15 is always the Feast of Unleavened Bread, and Nisan 16 is always the Feast of the First Fruits. No matter what day of the week these dates landed on, these three Sabbath Holidays always follow each other in sequence.

The personal, familial, Passover lamb would be sacrificed during as soon after sunset, the beginning of the 14th, as possible. The Seder meal would begin as soon as the families could begin. Note that Josephus says in the 1st century as many as 500,000 lambs had to be slaughtered to support all the visitors in Jerusalem.

Imagine, you're a family of 7 or 8 people, you take your lamb to the temple and line up the afternoon / evening of the 13th of Nisan. You wait in long lines to see a Priest. As soon as the sun set, ending 13 Nisan, and starting 14 Nisan – Passover – the lines would all start moving. You would lay your hands on the head of your lamb, the Priest could cut its throat and collect blood in a special bowl, then throw the blood on the alter. Your lamb is then hung on a hook and cleaned there at the temple grounds. Offering sacrifice for sin is a dirty business, to gain forgiveness for the dirty business of sin. Once done, you took the lamb carcass home and began preparing the Seder. It was not uncommon for this meal to not begin until well after what we as Westerners think of as 'midnight'.

Jews celebrate the Seder meal well after sunset on the 14th, eating the roasted lamb with matzah (unleavened bread) and bitter herbs. Before Passover begins, households conduct a ceremonial search for leaven (**bedikat chametz**) and remove all leavened products from their homes. During the Seder, participants drink four cups of wine and read from the Haggadah, which recounts the Exodus story.

Remember that God designed this Holiday to land on a full moon. That's an important detail to remember as we continue on. Is it any wonder that Jesus, though he sent his Apostles ahead, may not have begun his Seder meal until 11pm or midnight, or later? Eat from midnight to 2 am, then Peter, James and John are sleepy in the garden at 3am or so? This is partially my speculation, but I believe it is consistent with scripture.

The following morning, on the daytime part of 14 Nisan, the priests would go about offering their 2 normal *Tamid* sacrifices. In the context of Jewish sacrificial practice, *Tamid* (תָּמִיד) refers to the *daily burnt offering* that was performed in the Temple—one in the morning and one in the evening—without fail, every single day, 365 days a year. A lamb was offered for the people at roughly 9am, and another lamb was offered for the people at nearly precisely 3pm. On a Holy Holiday Sabbath, like Passover, those usual sacrifices would have taken place. On that special day, however, those *Tamid* sacrifices took on special meaning. The morning was the usual people's burnt offering. The afternoon, however, became the ***paschal lamb***.

This *paschal* lamb became a "korban", or an offering of atonement for the whole nation of Israel's sins. In Jewish tradition, ***korban*** (קָרְבָּן) refers to a sacrifice or offering brought to the Tabernacle or Temple as an act of worship, especially atonement and dedication to God.

The "Feast of Unleavened Bread" then begins at sunset, which marks the start of the 15th of Nisan by Jewish reckoning. However, both terms are commonly used interchangeably to describe the entire festival throughout the Talmud (Rabbinical writings), and are fairly confusing in the Old Testament prophets. What is Jewish law fact is the Passover was the 14th, the Feast of Unleavened Bread was the 15th, and the Harvest of the First Fruits was the 16th. Four more days of paschal festival, unleavened bread, and first early harvest were then celebrated.

The Biblical account makes it appear that the 14th of Nisan landed on a Friday the year that Jesus was crucified. To keep your minds straight, that means it began on your "Thursday night after sunset". Many writers have made a case that 14 Nisan could have fallen on a Friday only in certain years like 30 A.D. or 33 A.D. This is based on our understanding of the early Julian calendar.

The dating of Jesus' crucifixion to either 30 AD or 33 AD is supported by various biblical scholars and historians based on several converging lines of evidence. Here's what these scholars rely on:

Scholars Supporting 30 AD or 33 AD Dating

Scholars favoring 30 AD include:

- Colin Humphreys (Cambridge University)

- Jack Finegan (in "Handbook of Biblical Chronology")

- Andreas Köstenberger (theological scholar)

- Harold Hoehner (in "Chronological Aspects of the Life of Christ")

Scholars favoring 33 AD include:

- Sir Robert Anderson (in "The Coming Prince")

- William Lane Craig (philosopher and theologian)

- N.T. Wright (prominent New Testament scholar)

- Craig Blomberg (New Testament scholar)

- FF Bruce (New Testament Scholar)

Evidence Used for Dating

These scholars base their conclusions on several key factors:

1. **Pontius Pilate's governorship**: Historical records confirm Pilate was prefect of Judea from 26-36 AD, providing the outer boundaries.

2. **Astronomical calculations**: The crucifixion occurred on a Friday that was either Passover (14 Nisan) or the day before Passover, depending on which Gospel account is emphasized. Astronomers have calculated possible dates when 14 Nisan fell on or near Friday:

   o In 30 AD: Friday, April 7 (possible date)

   o In 33 AD: Friday, April 3 (possible date)

3. **John the Baptist's ministry**: Luke 3:1-2 dates the beginning of John's ministry to "the fifteenth year of the reign of Tiberius Caesar," which most scholars place around 28-29 AD. Jesus' ministry began shortly after.

4. **Length of Jesus' ministry**: John's Gospel mentions at least three Passovers during Jesus' ministry (possibly four), suggesting a 2-3 year ministry. If it began around 28 AD, this points to 30 or 33 AD for the crucifixion.

5. **The "fifteenth year of Tiberius"**: Scholarly debate exists on whether to count from when Tiberius became co-regent with Augustus (12 AD) or sole emperor (14 AD), yielding different potential start dates for Jesus' ministry.

6. **Lunar eclipse evidence**: Some scholars note Josephus mentioned a lunar eclipse before Herod's death, and astronomical records confirm such an eclipse in 4 BC, helping establish chronology.

Both the 30 AD and 33 AD dates have their strengths and challenges. The 33 AD date allows for a longer ministry and better aligns with some astronomical calculations, while the 30 AD date fits better with certain interpretations of when Jesus began his ministry relative to Tiberius's reign.

The scholarly consensus remains divided, though 30 AD and 33 AD have emerged as the most plausible candidates based on the available historical, biblical, and astronomical evidence.

Select Study: Peter's Influence on Mark

The Petrine Connection: Evidence for Peter's Role in Mark's Gospel

The Gospel of Mark has long been considered distinctive among the four canonical gospels for its vivid, action-oriented narrative style. While traditionally attributed to John Mark, compelling evidence suggests that the apostle Peter played a significant role in shaping this account of Jesus' life and ministry. This connection helps explain both the Gospel's unique characteristics and its apostolic authority despite being written by someone who was not one of the Twelve.

Historical Connections Between Peter and Mark

Their Personal Relationship

The New Testament provides several points of connection between Peter and John Mark that suggest a close relationship:

1. **Mark's Mother's House as Peter's Base** - Acts 12:12-17 records that when Peter was miraculously released from prison, "he went to the house of Mary, the mother of John who was

also called Mark, where many were gathered together and were praying." This indicates that Peter was familiar enough with Mark's family home to go there immediately after his escape. The text also suggests this home was a regular meeting place for the Jerusalem believers.

2. **Time Together in Jerusalem** - The timing of this prison release (around 44 AD) coincides approximately with when Mark returned to Jerusalem after departing from Paul and Barnabas during the First Missionary Journey (Acts 13:13). This means both Peter and Mark were in Jerusalem during the same period, providing opportunity for close collaboration.

3. **Peter's Reference to Mark as "My Son"** - In 1 Peter 5:13, Peter writes, "She who is in Babylon, chosen together with you, sends you greetings, and so does Mark, my son." This term of endearment suggests a close spiritual relationship between the two men. It is a mentoring relationship.

The Early Church Testimony

Beyond biblical evidence, early church fathers consistently connect Mark's Gospel with Peter:

1. **Papias (early 2nd century)** - In fragments preserved by Eusebius, Papias writes: "Mark, having become the interpreter of Peter, wrote down accurately, though not in order, whatsoever he remembered of the things said or done by Christ... Mark made no mistake... for he was careful of one thing, not to omit any of the things he had heard, and not to state any of them falsely."

2. **Irenaeus (late 2nd century)** - States that "after their (Peter and Paul's) departure, Mark, the disciple and interpreter of Peter, did also hand down to us in writing what had been preached by Peter."

3. **Clement of Alexandria** - Reports that Mark wrote at the request of Christians in Rome who wanted a written record of Peter's oral teachings.

Textual Evidence Within Mark's Gospel

The Gospel itself contains internal evidence suggesting Peter's influence:

Eyewitness Perspective

1. **Vivid Details** - Mark's Gospel contains numerous instances of precise, vivid details that suggest firsthand observation. For example, the

detail that Jesus was "in the stern, asleep on the cushion" during the storm (Mark 4:38), or that the grass was "green" when Jesus fed the five thousand (Mark 6:39). These details align with what we would expect from Peter's eyewitness accounts.

2. **Focus on Action** - The frequent use of the word "immediately" (over 40 times) gives the narrative an urgent, eyewitness quality consistent with Peter's impulsive personality.

Petrine Emphasis and Perspective

1. **Peter's Prominence** - Peter is mentioned more frequently in Mark than in other gospels, often appearing at key moments. The Gospel begins with Peter's call (1:16-18) and contains detailed accounts of Peter's experiences, including his confession, rebuke, denial, and restoration.

2. **Peter's Failures** - Interestingly, Mark does not gloss over Peter's failures and is sometimes more critical of the disciple than other gospels. This unflattering portrayal suggests the humility of Peter in acknowledging his own shortcomings— something unlikely to be fabricated by someone writing without Peter's input.

3. **Omission of Peter's Special Recognition** -
   Mark omits some incidents that highlight Peter's
   special status, such as Jesus' words in Matthew
   16:17-19 after Peter's confession. This could
   reflect Peter's humility in not emphasizing his
   own importance when relating events to Mark.

Thematic Connections

The Servant Theme

One of the most striking connections between Peter's
preaching in Acts and Mark's Gospel is the shared
emphasis on Jesus as servant:

1. **Mark's Emphasis** - Mark 10:45 contains the key
   verse that encapsulates the Gospel's portrait of
   Jesus: "For even the Son of Man did not come to
   be served, but to serve, and to give his life as a
   ransom for many." This theme of servanthood
   runs throughout the Gospel.

2. **Peter's Preaching** - In Acts 3:13 and 3:26, Peter
   refers explicitly to Jesus as God's "Servant"
   (παῖδα, pais), echoing Isaiah's Servant Songs. This
   term is rarely used for Jesus in the New
   Testament outside these contexts, creating a
   distinctive thematic link between Peter's
   preaching and the Gospel of Mark.

Focus on Action and Power

Both Peter's preaching in Acts and Mark's Gospel emphasize:

1. **Jesus' Deeds** - Peter in Acts 10:38 summarizes Jesus' ministry as "going about doing good and healing all who were oppressed by the devil." This action-oriented summary perfectly captures Mark's portrayal of Jesus, who is constantly on the move performing miracles and confronting evil.

2. **The Cross and Resurrection** - Both Peter's sermons and Mark's Gospel build toward the crucifixion and resurrection as the climactic events of Jesus' ministry.

Linguistic and Stylistic Connections

1. **Simple Language** - Mark's Greek is relatively simple and direct, similar to the straightforward style we might expect from Peter, a Galilean fisherman. The Gospel lacks the more sophisticated Greek constructions found in Luke or the theological complexity of John.

2. **Aramaic Preservation** - Mark uniquely preserves several Aramaic phrases spoken by Jesus (such as "Talitha kum" in 5:41), translating them for his

audience. This suggests a source (like Peter) who remembered Jesus' actual Aramaic words and shared them with the author.

Internal Consistency Between Mark's Gospel and Peter's Epistles

Beyond the connections already explored, there are striking parallels in theology, language, and thematic concerns between Mark's Gospel and the Petrine epistles, further supporting Peter's influence on Mark:

Theological Parallels

1. **Christology** - Both Mark and Peter's epistles present Christ as the suffering servant who also possesses divine authority. Mark portrays Jesus as one who "taught as one having authority" (Mark 1:22) while simultaneously highlighting his suffering. Similarly, 1 Peter emphasizes Christ's suffering (1 Peter 2:21-25) while affirming his lordship (1 Peter 3:22).

2. **The Cross and Discipleship** - In Mark 8:34-38, Jesus calls disciples to take up their cross and follow him. This same theology of suffering as the path of discipleship appears in 1 Peter 2:21: "For to this you have been called, because Christ also suffered for you, leaving you an example, so that you might follow in his steps."

3. **Ransom Theology** - Mark's key verse (10:45) describes Jesus giving "his life as a ransom for many." 1 Peter 1:18-19 employs similar redemptive language: "you were ransomed from the futile ways inherited from your forefathers, not with perishable things such as silver or gold, but with the precious blood of Christ."

Linguistic and Conceptual Similarities

1. **Eyewitness Emphasis** - 2 Peter 1:16 states, "For we did not follow cleverly devised myths when we made known to you the power and coming of our Lord Jesus Christ, but we were eyewitnesses of his majesty." This emphasis on eyewitness testimony aligns with Mark's vivid, detail-rich narrative style.

2. **Common Terminology** - Both use the term "Gospel" (εὐαγγέλιον) in similar ways. Mark begins with "The beginning of the gospel of Jesus Christ" (Mark 1:1), while 1 Peter refers to those "who preached the good news (gospel) to you" (1 Peter 1:12).

3. **Eschatological Urgency** - Mark's Gospel conveys an urgency about the kingdom of God (Mark 1:15), which is mirrored in 1 Peter's expectation of imminent judgment: "The end of all things is at hand" (1 Peter 4:7).

Shared Imagery and References

1. **Shepherd Imagery** - Mark records Jesus' words about the shepherd being struck and the sheep scattered (Mark 14:27). Peter develops this shepherd metaphor in 1 Peter 2:25: "For you were straying like sheep, but have now returned to the Shepherd and Overseer of your souls."

2. **Stone/Cornerstone References** - Mark records Jesus' citation of Psalm 118:22 regarding the rejected stone becoming the cornerstone (Mark 12:10-11). Peter uses this same reference prominently in 1 Peter 2:7.

3. **The Transfiguration** - While Mark records the Transfiguration (Mark 9:2-8), 2 Peter 1:16-18 explicitly references this event as a personal memory, directly linking Peter's experience and Mark's account.

Distinctive Approaches to Suffering

Both Mark's Gospel and 1 Peter have a distinctive focus on the theme of suffering:

1. Mark devotes proportionally more text to Jesus' passion than the other Gospels.

2. 1 Peter contains more references to suffering (in relation to its length) than any other New Testament epistle.

3. Both connect suffering with divine purpose and vindication.

These parallels strengthen the case for Petrine influence on Mark's Gospel, as they demonstrate consistency in theological perspective, language, and thematic concerns that would be expected if Mark were indeed preserving and organizing Peter's testimony about Jesus.

As one of the earliest gospel accounts, Mark's work not only reflects an individual perspective but also bears the weight of Peter's apostolic testimony.

The Gospel of Mark stands as a testament to early Christian collaboration, where the experiences of an apostle who walked with Jesus (Peter) were preserved by a second believer who was not part of Jesus' inner circle during His lifetime (Mark). This relationship helps explain how the vivid, action-oriented account that focuses on Jesus as servant came to be written—a Gospel that bears the marks of both an eyewitness perspective and a carefully crafted narrative designed to communicate the good news to a broader audience.

Select Study: Jesus the Paschal Lamb

Jesus the Paschal Lamb

"Behold, the Lamb of God, who takes away the sin of the world!" (John 1:29)

These words, proclaimed by John the Baptist as Jesus approached the Jordan River, would have resonated deeply with every Jewish listener. They understood lambs. They understood sacrifice. They understood Passover. What they could not yet fully comprehend was how the man walking toward them would fulfill every detail of a ritual their ancestors had observed for over a millennium. The precision with which Christ's final week aligned with the Passover celebration reveals a divine orchestration that transforms our understanding of both the ancient feast and the crucifixion itself.

To appreciate this profound connection, we must first understand how God established time itself in the Hebrew mindset, then trace the thread of the Paschal lamb from Egypt to Golgotha.

The Hebrew Understanding of Time

Days Begin at Evening

In the Genesis account of creation, we encounter a pattern that would shape Jewish timekeeping forever: "And there was evening and there was morning, the first day" (Genesis 1:5). This phrase repeats throughout the creation narrative (Genesis 1:8, 13, 19, 23, 31), establishing that in God's economy, days begin at sunset, not sunrise.

The Hebrew words themselves reveal this understanding:

- עֶרֶב (*'ereb*, H6153) - dusk, evening, the beginning of the day

- בֹּקֶר (*bôqer*, H1242) - dawn, morning, the breaking of day

This concept is crucial for understanding the timeline of Christ's passion. When the Gospels speak of preparation day and the Sabbath, they refer to periods beginning at sunset, not midnight as in our modern reckoning. Every authoritative Jewish source confirms that sunset marks the end of one day and the beginning of the next—a perspective we must adopt to understand the Passover narrative.

The Sabbath Rest

"Six days you shall labor, and do all your work, but the seventh day is a Sabbath to the LORD your God" (Exodus 20:9-10). The Hebrew word שַׁבָּת (*shabbâth*, H7676) means "intermission" or "rest." This weekly rhythm, established at creation and codified at Sinai, would play a critical role in the timing of Christ's death and resurrection.

Importantly, the day following Passover was always treated as a special Sabbath, regardless of which day of the week it fell upon. Leviticus 23:7 commands: "On the first day you shall have a holy convocation; you shall not do any ordinary work." When this Holy Holiday landed on the 7th day of the week, it was treated as a special sabbath. This "High Sabbath" or "High Holy Day" is what John references when he notes that the Jewish leaders wanted the bodies removed from the crosses "for that Sabbath was a high day" (John 19:31). When the Feast of Unleavened Bread happened to fall on a weekly Sabbath, it became a High Holy Sabbath.

The Month of New Beginnings

Abib: The Month of Green Ears

God designated a specific month for the Exodus and, prophetically, for our redemption: "This month shall be for you the beginning of months. It shall be the first month of the year for you" (Exodus 12:2). This month was called אָבִיב ('âbîyb, H24), meaning "green ears of grain," referring to the barley being in the ear but still green.

The timing was agricultural and theological simultaneously. Exodus 9:31 notes, "The flax and the barley were struck down, for the barley was in the ear and the flax was in bud." This agricultural marker ensured that Passover would always occur in spring, the season of new life and new beginnings.

The Hebrew word for month, חֹדֶשׁ (chôdesh, H2320), literally means "new moon," as months in the Jewish calendar begin with the new moon. Passover always occurs at the full moon, when the night sky provides maximum illumination—a practical provision for a feast that would involve nighttime travel and activity.

The Original Passover

Selection and Examination

"Tell all the congregation of Israel that on the tenth day of this month every man shall take a lamb according to their fathers' houses, a lamb for a household" (Exodus 12:3). The lamb was not chosen hastily. Each family selected their lamb four days before Passover, bringing it into their home. During these four days, they would examine it carefully, ensuring it met God's requirements:

"Your lamb shall be without blemish, a male a year old" (Exodus 12:5).

This four-day examination period was not arbitrary. It allowed the family to verify the lamb's perfection while also forming an attachment to the animal, making its sacrifice more poignant. The lamb became, temporarily, part of the household—making its death a substitutionary act rather than a mere ritual.

The Sacrifice

"You shall keep it until the fourteenth day of this month, when the whole assembly of the congregation of Israel shall kill their lambs at twilight" (Exodus 12:6). The Hebrew phrase translated "at twilight" literally means "between the evenings"—the time between the sun's decline and sunset, approximately 3:00 to 6:00 PM.

The instructions were specific and significant:

- The blood must be applied to the doorposts and lintel (Exodus 12:7)

- The lamb must be roasted with fire, not boiled (Exodus 12:8-9)

- It must be eaten with unleavened bread and bitter herbs (Exodus 12:8)

- Not one of its bones could be broken (Exodus 12:46)

- Nothing could remain until morning (Exodus 12:10)

Each detail carried meaning that would find ultimate fulfillment in Christ.

Let us make sure we understand this. In the afternoon of the 13th of Nisan, the people of Israel would line up, preparing to sacrifice their personal familial lambs. As soon as the sun dropped below the horizon, they would begin sacrificing their family's Passover lambs. This is the first few hours of Passover, the 14th of Nisan. In the original sacrifice in Egypt, they spread blood on the doorposts, and ate standing through the night, awaiting the end of God's spirit passing over the people. In the early morning hours, they fled Egypt.

Christ's Final Week: The Greater Exodus

Six Days Before: Preparation for Burial

John's Gospel provides a crucial timestamp: "Six days before the Passover, Jesus therefore came to Bethany" (John 12:1). This would place Jesus' arrival on the 8th of Nisan. That evening, Mary of Bethany performed an act of devotion that Jesus interpreted prophetically: "She has kept it for the day of my burial" (John 12:7).

The expensive nard that filled the house with fragrance was burial spice. Unknown to most present, Jesus was already being prepared for death. The Lamb of God was being anointed for sacrifice before He was even selected by Israel.

The Tenth of Nisan: The Lamb Enters the Home

"The next day the large crowd that had come to the feast heard that Jesus was coming to Jerusalem" (John 12:12). On the very day when every Jewish household was about to select their Passover lamb, Jesus entered Jerusalem to the cries of "Hosanna! Blessed is he who comes in the name of the Lord, even the King of Israel!" (John 12:13).

The parallel is unmistakable. As thousands and thousands of lambs were being brought into Jerusalem, entering at the Sheep's Gate on the 9th of Nisan, Jews who were buying their lambs in Jerusalem were lining up at the temple mount. It's in the middle of this pandemonium of sheep that Jesus also entered by the Sheep's Gate, riding on a donkey. It is the same afternoon and ends the same way at twilight. Jewish homes throughout Jerusalem, a command we just studied from Exodus 12:3, the Lamb of God was being brought into the house of Israel. Every household was inspecting their lamb right after twilight, the start of the 10th of Nisan, starting the 4 days of ensuring its perfection, and becoming attached to the animal that would redeem them. On this exact day, at this same time, the palm branches, the cries of acclaim, the prophetic fulfillment of Zechariah 9:9—all marked this as Israel's unconscious selection of their Paschal Lamb – Jesus the Christ.

Yes, Jesus chose to enter Jerusalem, for his "Triumphal Entry" through the Lamb's Gate – not the King's Gate. The Lamb's Gate is at the obscure far northeast corner of Jerusalem, off the road from Bethany. This gate was used mainly for travelers, but at Passover, it was used to bring all the sacrificial animals into the city, to the Temple Mount. Imagine hundreds of thousands of sheep, adoring worshippers, and Jesus, entering Jerusalem, four days before Passover.

Days of Examination

Just as the Passover lamb underwent four days of examination, Jesus spent His final days being scrutinized by every religious and political authority:

Day One (10th of Nisan): Jesus cleanses the Temple, directly challenging the religious establishment (Matthew 21:12-13). His actions fulfill Malachi 3:1-3, as the Lord suddenly comes to His temple for purification.

Day Two (11th of Nisan): The chief priests, scribes, and elders challenge His authority (Mark 11:27-33). They examine His credentials but cannot find fault with His answers.

Day Three (12th of Nisan): A day of intensive examination:

- The Pharisees and Herodians test Him about taxes (Matthew 22:15-22)

- The Sadducees challenge Him about resurrection (Matthew 22:23-33)

- A lawyer tests Him about the greatest commandment (Matthew 22:34-40)

Day Four (13th of Nisan): Jesus teaches extensively, pronouncing woes upon the religious leaders (Matthew 23) and delivering the Olivet Discourse (Matthew 24-25). The examination concludes with the authorities finding no legitimate charge against Him, fulfilling the requirement that the lamb be "without blemish."

Passover Night: The New Covenant

As the sun set on the 13th of Nisan, the 14th began—Passover proper. Luke records Jesus' words: "I have earnestly desired to eat this Passover with you before I suffer" (Luke 22:15). Some commentaries struggle with the timeline, trying to put the personal family Passover meal after the Paschal sacrifice on the afternoon of the 14th of Nisan. That's not what happened. Right after sunset begins the 14th of Nisan, families had their lambs executed on the Temple Mount and began their personal

Passover Seder. We'll see in a little bit that on the afternoon of the 14th of Nisan, the Priests would offer the National Paschal Lamb. During this personal meal, Jesus transformed the ancient ritual:

The Bread: "This is my body, which is given for you" (Luke 22:19). The unleavened bread, representing the haste of exodus and the absence of corruption, became a symbol of His sinless body.

The Cup: Among the four traditional cups of Passover:

1. The Cup of Blessing ("I will deliver you")

2. The Cup of Judgment ("I will free you")

3. The Cup of Redemption ("I will redeem you with an outstretched arm")

4. The Cup of Praise ("I will take you as my own people")

Jesus took the third cup, the Cup of Redemption, saying, "This cup that is poured out for you is the new covenant in my blood" (Luke 22:20).

The Night of Agony

Following the meal, the events unfolded rapidly:

- Prayer in Gethsemane (Matthew 26:36-46)

- Betrayal and arrest (John 18:2-12)

- Trial before Annas (John 18:13-14)

- Trial before Caiaphas (John 18:24)

- Peter's denial (John 18:15-27)

- Trial before the Sanhedrin at daybreak (Luke 22:66-71)

How could all this activity occur at night? Remember that Passover always falls at the full moon, providing natural illumination for the proceedings. God's cosmic timing ensured sufficient light for the dark deeds of that night.

The Day of Sacrifice

The Third Hour: The Morning Sacrifice

"And it was the third hour when they crucified him" (Mark 15:25). The third hour—9:00 AM by Jewish reckoning—held special significance in Temple worship. This was when the first daily sacrifice (*Tamid*) was offered. The Mishnah records that on feast days, the Temple bells would ring and the priests would call all to worship (Mishnah Tamid 3:7).

As the first *Tamid* lamb of the day was being bound to the altar in the Temple, the Lamb of God was being nailed to the cross on Golgotha. The exactness of the time reveals divine orchestration.

If you were standing at the foot of the cross, you could hear the bells ring out and the shouts of praise for God as the Priests killed the *Tamid* lamb. If you were near the Temple court, you could hear the distinctive sound of an executioner's hammer, falling over and over, nailing a perfect man to the cross. These two places were very close together. If you were in the area, you could hear both.

Jesus is the paschal lamb of Israel.

Darkness at Noon

"Now from the sixth hour there was darkness over all the land until the ninth hour" (Matthew 27:45). From noon until 3:00 PM, supernatural darkness covered the land. This was not an eclipse—impossible during a full moon—but a divine sign. The sun, created on the fourth day to "rule over the day" (Genesis 1:16), abdicated its rule as the Light of the World hung dying.

The Ninth Hour: The Evening Sacrifice

"And about the ninth hour Jesus cried out with a loud voice, saying, 'Eli, Eli, lema sabachthani?' that is, 'My God, my God, why have you forsaken me?'" (Matthew 27:46, quoting Psalm 22, to a Jew, citing the first phrase of a passage or Psalm was designed to bring the whole text to remembrance). The ninth hour—3:00 PM—was the time of the evening sacrifice, when the second *tamid* lamb was offered. Bells were rung, and the shofar (ram's horn trumpet) was blown. Again, anyone near the cross or the temple could hear both – the shouts of the flawless savior, the bells, the trumpet, and the bleats of the national Paschal lamb for the people.

As this national paschal lamb was sacrificed, Jesus declared, "It is finished" (John 19:30) and "yielded up his spirit" (Matthew 27:50).

The very moment when the high priest slaughtered the official Passover lamb for the nation, our High Priest offered Himself as the final Passover Lamb; Jesus the Christ, the Lamb of God who takes away the sin of the world. The earthly shadow gave way to the heavenly reality.

The Torn Veil

"And behold, the curtain of the temple was torn in two, from top to bottom" (Matthew 27:51). This massive curtain, according to Jewish sources, was 60 feet high and 4 inches thick. Its supernatural tearing from top to bottom—impossible by human hands—occurred at the very moment of the evening sacrifice.

The priests offering the Passover lamb would have witnessed this unprecedented event. The veil that had separated the Holy of Holies, entered only once a year with the blood of atonement, was suddenly opened. The way into God's presence, long barred by sin, was now accessible through the blood of the perfect Lamb.

Prophetic Fulfillments

Not a Bone Broken

The Roman soldiers, seeking to hasten death before the Sabbath, came to break the legs of the crucified. "But when they came to Jesus and saw that he was already dead, they did not break his legs" (John 19:33). John explicitly connects this to two prophecies:

- The Passover regulation: "you shall not break any of its bones" (Exodus 12:46)

- The Messianic psalm: "He keeps all his bones; not one of them is broken" (Psalm 34:20)

Even Roman executioners, unaware of Jewish law, fulfilled divine prophecy. The Lamb of God remained unblemished even in death.

The True Sabbath Rest

Jesus' body was hastily placed in the tomb before sunset on Passover, as the High Sabbath was beginning. He rested in the tomb throughout this special Sabbath—the 15th of Nisan, the Feast of Unleavened Bread. The One who said, "Come to me, all who labor and are heavy laden, and I will give you rest" (Matthew 11:28) was Himself resting from His completed work of redemption.

First Fruits of Resurrection

"On the day after the Sabbath the priest shall wave it" (Leviticus 23:11). The Feast of First Fruits occurred on the day after the Fest of Unleavened Bread following Passover. On this very day, "up from the grave He arose," becoming "the firstfruits of those who have fallen asleep" (1 Corinthians 15:20).

The agricultural festival celebrating the first of the harvest became the celebration of the first resurrection from the dead, promising a full harvest to come.

Theological Implications

The Greater Exodus

The Passover commemorated Israel's deliverance from slavery in Egypt. Christ's death accomplished a greater exodus—deliverance from slavery to sin. As Paul writes, "Christ, our Passover lamb, has been sacrificed" (1 Corinthians 5:7).

The parallels extend throughout:

- Blood on the doorposts protected from death; Christ's blood protects from eternal death

- Unleavened bread represented purity; Christ was without the leaven of sin

- All Jewish homes cleansed themselves from leaven to prepare for Passover; Jesus cleansed the temple, freeing it from the leaven of the Pharisees (Matt 16:6)

- Bitter herbs recalled the bitterness of slavery; Christ tasted the bitterness of our sin.

- The lamb's flesh provided strength for the journey; Christ's flesh gives us strength for our spiritual journey.

- The hasty departure from Egypt; our urgent call to leave the kingdom of darkness

Personal Application

Understanding Jesus as our Paschal Lamb transforms
how we approach both the Old Testament feasts and the
New Testament fulfillment. We see that:

1. **God's timing is perfect.** The precision of
   Christ's passion week reveals a God who
   orchestrates history down to the hour. We can
   trust His timing in our lives.

2. **Symbols find their substance in Christ.** Every
   detail of the Passover ritual pointed forward to
   Jesus. The shadows of the Old Covenant help us
   appreciate the reality of the New.

3. **Examination precedes acceptance.** Just as the
   Passover lamb was examined for four days, we are
   called to examine Christ's claims carefully. Faith is
   not blind but based on thorough investigation.

4. **Sacrifice requires substitution.** The lamb died
   so the firstborn could live. Christ died so we
   could have eternal life. Salvation has always been
   through substitutionary sacrifice.

5. **Deliverance demands departure.** Israel could
   not remain in Egypt after Passover. We cannot
   remain in our old life after accepting Christ's
   sacrifice.

Conclusion

When John the Baptist declared, "Behold, the Lamb of God," he was announcing the culmination of fifteen centuries of Passover observance. Every lamb sacrificed since that night in Egypt had pointed forward to this moment. Every drop of blood on Jewish doorposts anticipated the blood that would flow from Calvary's cross.

The precision of the fulfillment—from the selection on the 10th of Nisan to the resurrection on First Fruits—reveals not coincidence but divine design. Christ did not merely die during Passover week; He fulfilled Passover in every detail. He is not just like the Passover lamb; He is the reality to which all Passover lambs pointed.

Today, when we partake of Communion, we participate in this same reality. We proclaim that the Lamb who was slain before the foundation of the world has accomplished our eternal exodus from sin and death.

Simply tell the greatest story ever told. Experience it first-hand from the Gospel 'closest to where you are.' Never underestimate the power in that simplicity. The Lamb of God who takes away the sin of the world invites us to apply His blood to the doorposts of our hearts, to feast on His sacrifice, and to prepare for our journey to the Promised Land.

"For indeed Christ, our Passover, was sacrificed for us. Therefore let us keep the feast, not with old leaven, nor with the leaven of malice and wickedness, but with the unleavened bread of sincerity and truth" (1 Corinthians 5:7-8).

"Worthy is the Lamb who was slain, to receive power and wealth and wisdom and might and honor and glory and blessing!" (Revelation 5:12)

Select Study: Silences of John

The Strategic Silences of John

"And there are also many other things that Jesus did, which if they were written one by one, I suppose that even the world itself could not contain the books that would be written" (John 21:25).

With these words, John acknowledges what every reader of his Gospel eventually discovers: he has deliberately omitted much that the other Gospel writers included. Far from being oversights or deficiencies, these omissions reveal John's distinct theological purpose. What John leaves unsaid speaks as powerfully as what he proclaims. His silences are strategic, his absences intentional, all serving to present Jesus as the eternal Word made flesh, the divine Son who reveals the Father.

The Missing Biography

No Genealogy, No Nativity

While Matthew traces Jesus' lineage to Abraham and Luke to Adam, John begins before time itself: "In the beginning was the Word" (John 1:1). John has no interest in earthly ancestry when presenting One whose origin is eternal. Similarly, he omits the nativity narrative entirely. No manger, no shepherds, no wise men. For John, the pivotal moment is not birth in Bethlehem but the Word becoming flesh (John 1:14).

The Silent Mother

Mary appears in John's Gospel but remains nameless. Jesus addresses her not as "Mother" but as "Woman" (John 2:4; 19:26). This is not disrespect but theological precision—John emphasizes Jesus' divine relationships over human ones. Even His brothers remain unnamed, though their unbelief is noted (John 7:5).

Missing Milestones

John omits Jesus' baptism entirely, though he records John the Baptist's testimony about it (John 1:32-34). The temptation in the wilderness never appears. Satan receives only one mention (John 13:27) compared to fifteen in the Synoptics. John's Jesus needs no testing to prove His divine sonship—it is self-evident from the beginning.

The Absent Teachings

No Parables

The Synoptics overflow with parables—earthly stories with heavenly meanings. John records none. Instead of "The kingdom of heaven is like..." John gives us "I AM..." statements. Rather than indirect teaching through stories,

John's Jesus speaks directly: "I am the bread of life" (John 6:35), "I am the light of the world" (John 8:12).

Major Discourses Missing

The Sermon on the Mount, that charter of kingdom living, appears nowhere in John. The Olivet Discourse about the end times is absent. The missionary instructions to the Twelve are omitted. Instead, John provides extended dialogues at the Last Supper (John 13-17), theological discussions with Nicodemus (John 3) and the Samaritan woman (John 4).

The Lord's Prayer Unrecorded

"Our Father who art in heaven..." These beloved words taught to the disciples are missing from John. Instead, John gives us Jesus' High Priestly Prayer (John 17), where we overhear the Son speaking directly to the Father, not teaching others how to pray but demonstrating the intimate communion of the Trinity.

The Different Miracles

No Exorcisms

While the Synoptics frequently show Jesus casting out demons, John records not a single exorcism. The word "demon" appears only in accusations against Jesus (John 7:20; 8:48-52; 10:20-21). John's focus is not on Jesus' power over evil spirits but His authority as the source of life itself.

Selected Signs

John carefully chooses seven signs before the resurrection, each revealing Jesus' divine nature. He omits the healing of lepers, the cleansing that marked the messianic arrival. He excludes the second feeding of the multitude. Every miracle in John serves as a sign pointing to Jesus' identity rather than merely demonstrating compassion or power.

The Passion Differences

No Agony in Gethsemane

The Synoptics describe Jesus' anguish, sweating blood, pleading for the cup to pass. John shows no such struggle. His Jesus prays calmly, extensively, focusing on glorifying the Father and protecting the disciples (John 17). The divine Son who laid down His life voluntarily (John 10:18) needs no agonizing deliberation.

Missing Details of Suffering

John omits:

- The kiss of Judas (though Judas is present)

- Simon of Cyrene carrying the cross

- The cry "My God, why have you forsaken me?"

- The promise to the repentant thief

- "Father, forgive them..."

- The darkness and earthquake at Jesus' death

Instead, John emphasizes Jesus' control: "It is finished" (John 19:30)—a cry not of defeat but accomplishment.

No Formal Trial

While the Synoptics detail the Sanhedrin trial, John focuses on the private interrogations before Annas and Pilate. The theological debates that run throughout John's Gospel serve as Jesus' real trial, where He is repeatedly judged and rejected by "His own" (John 1:11).

The Missing Themes

Kingdom Language Minimized

"Kingdom of God" appears only twice in John (3:3, 5) versus over 100 times in the Synoptics. John emphasizes eternal life, which is mentioned 17 times in John, compared to 26 times in all three Synoptics. The shift is from future kingdom to present relationship.

Absence of Key Terms

Faith: The noun never appears in John, though the verb "believe" appears 98 times. John emphasizes active believing over static faith.

Repentance: Never mentioned. John focuses on believing and receiving rather than turning and changing.

Forgiveness: The word group appears once (John 20:23) versus dozens of times in the Synoptics. John emphasizes life over pardon.

Gospel: The word never appears. John IS the Gospel, not merely proclaiming it.

Compassion: Not mentioned once. John shows Jesus' love through laying down His life, not through emotional responses.

Different Ethical Focus

John records no teaching about:

- Loving enemies

- Divorce

- Render unto Caesar

- Woes against Pharisees

Instead, John emphasizes one command: "Love one another as I have loved you" (John 13:34). The ethics flow from a relationship with Christ, not from moral instruction.

The Theological Purpose

These omissions reveal John's purpose: presenting Jesus as the divine Son who perfectly reveals the Father. Every deletion serves this goal:

- Genealogies would emphasize human origin over divine nature

- Parables would veil what John wants to reveal directly

- Exorcisms would focus on the enemy rather than the Savior

- Kingdom language might perpetuate Jewish political expectations

- Ethical teaching could overshadow the essential relationship

John strips away everything that might distract from his central message: Jesus is the Christ, the Son of God, and by believing you may have life in His name (John 20:31).

What Only John Records

To understand John's omissions, we must see what he alone includes:

Theological Foundations:

- The Prologue: Word became flesh (1:1-18)

- Seven "I AM" statements

- Jesus' pre-existence and divine glory

Unique Miracles:

- Water to wine at Cana (2:1-11)

- Healing at the Pool of Bethesda (5:1-15)

- Man born blind (9:1-41)

- Raising of Lazarus (11:1-44)

Private Conversations:

- Nicodemus at night (3:1-21)

- Samaritan woman at the well (4:1-42)

- Extended Last Supper discourse (13-17)

Distinctive Events:

- Foot washing (13:1-17)

- Jesus' High Priestly Prayer (17:1-26)

- Blood and water from Jesus' side (19:34)

- Restoration of Peter (21:15-19)

Unique Themes:

- Jesus as fulfillment of Jewish festivals

- The witness theme (over 40 times)

- The Paraclete/Holy Spirit teaching (14-16)

- Mutual indwelling of Father and Son

- "Hour" of glorification

Post-Resurrection Appearances:

- Mary Magdalene alone at the tomb (20:11-18)

- Thomas's doubt and confession (20:24-29)

- Seaside breakfast and catch of 153 fish (21:1-14)

Conclusion

John's Gospel is not deficient but different, not lacking but laser-focused. His omissions create space for deeper theological reflection. By removing the familiar, he forces us to see Jesus anew—not as teacher, healer, or prophet primarily, but as the Word made flesh, the only begotten Son, the revelation of the invisible God.

The Synoptics give us the earthly Jesus moving toward His destiny. John gives us the heavenly Son who descended to reveal and redeem. The Synoptics show us what Jesus did and taught. John shows us who Jesus is.

Perhaps this is why John's Gospel has been called the spiritual Gospel since ancient times. His strategic silences invite us beyond historical facts to spiritual realities, beyond earthly ministry to eternal significance, beyond knowing about Jesus to knowing Jesus Himself.

"These are written that you may believe that Jesus is the Christ, the Son of God, and that believing you may have life in His name" (John 20:31). Everything included serves this purpose. Everything omitted would have distracted from it. In John's Gospel, less becomes more as absence amplifies presence—the presence of the Word who was with God and was God, dwelling among us, full of grace and truth.

Select Study: Blameless

The word 'blameless' appears in multiple translations in the context of Luke 1:6 to describe Elizabeth and Zechariah.

ASV Luke 1:6 "And they were both righteous before God, walking in all the commandments and ordinances of the Lord blameless."

KJV Luke 1:6 "And[1161] they were[2258] both[297] righteous[1342] before[1799] God,[2316] walking[4198] in[1722] all[3956] the[3588] commandments[1785] and[2532] ordinances[1345] of the[3588] Lord[2962] blameless.[273] "

The word 'blameless' is defined by Strong's as:

G273 ἄμεμπτος amemptos

am'-emp-tos From G1 (as a negative particle) and a derivative of G3201; *irreproachable:* - blameless, faultless, unblamable.

The word from which this is derived is:

G3201 μέμφομαι memphomai

mem'-fom-ahee Middle voice of an primary verb; to *blame:* - find fault.

Barnes has this to say about the use of the word blameless in this text:

Luk 1:6 -

Both righteous - Both "just" or holy. This means here more than external conformity to the law. It is an honorable testimonial of their "piety" toward God.

Walking in ... - Keeping the commandments. To walk in the way that God commands is "to obey."

Ordinances - Rites and customs which God had ordained or appointed. These words refer to all the duties of religion which were made known to them.

Blameless - That is, no fault or deficiency could be found in them. They were strict, exact, punctual. Yet this, if it had been mere "external" observance, might have been no proof of piety. Paul, before his conversion, also kept the law "externally" blameless, Phi 3:6. But in the case of Zechariah and Elizabeth it was real love to God and sincere regard for his law.

The word blameless is also used by the KJV in 1 Tim 3:2, but it comes from a different linguistic root.

KJV 1Tim 3:2 "A bishop[1985] then[3767] must[1163] be[1511] blameless,[423] the husband[435] of one[3391] wife,[1135] vigilant,[3524] sober,[4998] of good behavior,[2887] given to hospitality,[5382] apt to teach;[1317] "

In this case, the word translated as blameless is:

G423 ἀνεπίληπτος anepileptos

an-ep-eel'-ape-tos From G1 (as a negative particle) and a derivative of G1949; *not arrested*, that is, (by implication) *inculpable:* - blameless, unrebukeable.

And its root is:

G1949 ἐπιλαμβάνομαι epilambanomai

ep-ee-lam-ban'-om-ahee Middle voice from G1909 and G2983; to *seize* (for help, injury, attainment or any other purpose; literally or figuratively): - catch, lay hold (up-) on, take (by, hold of, on).

Which drives the need to look also to the following two additional root words:

G1909 ἐπί epi

ep-ee' A primary preposition properly meaning *superimposition* (of time, place, order, etc.), as a relation of *distribution* (with the genitive case), that is, *over, upon,* etc.; of *rest* (with the dative case) *at, on,* etc.; of *direction* (with the accusative case) *towards, upon,* etc.: - about (the times), above, after, against, among, as long as (touching), at, beside, X have charge of, (be-, (where-)) fore, in (a place, as much as, the time of, -to), (because) of, (up-) on (behalf of) over, (by, for) the space of, through (-out), (un-) to (-ward), with. In compounds it retains essentially the same import, *at*, *upon*, etc. (literally or figuratively).

And

G2983 λαμβάνω lambanō

lam-ban'-o A prolonged form of a primary verb, which is used only as an alternate in certain tenses; to *take* (in very many applications, literally and figuratively (probably objective or active, to *get hold* of; whereas G1209 is rather subjective or passive, to *have offered* to one; while G138 is more violent, to *seize* or *remove*)): - accept, + be amazed, assay, attain, bring, X when I call, catch, come on (X unto), + forget, have, hold, obtain, receive (X after), take (away, up).

From these definitions, it appears to me that the American Standard more rightly translates this verse in its use of the phrase 'without reproach,' and some translations render it 'above reproach.' From a review of the definitions, it appears that the rendering 'above reproach' implies an obedient righteousness, while 'blameless' implies legal compliance. Where blameless may be more a more thorough obedience, above reproach includes the concept of purpose as well as durability under scrutiny.

ASV 1Ti 3:2 *"The bishop therefore must be without reproach, the husband of one wife, temperate, sober-minded, orderly, given to hospitality, apt to teach;"*

It seems to me that the implication brought in Luke 1:6 and Phil 3:6 for blameless is one of higher accomplishment of the action of the law than what is implied in 1 Tim 3:2. In the case in Timothy, it appears the qualification of 'above reproach' is to be of such a relationship with the lifestyle of Christianity that bringing accusations against you is a pointless effort. This concept truly embodies the concept of 'irreproachable.' In the case of being blameless, there is a disparity between the way Luke uses it to describe Zechariah and Elizabeth, versus how Paul uses it to describe himself. Looking to Paul for clarification on this word:

ASV Phil 3:6 *"as touching zeal, persecuting the church; as touching the righteousness which is in the law, found blameless."*

Paul, in context of saying if he can have confidence in his own flesh and actions, describes himself as 'blameless.' He also describes himself as lost despite that seeming perfection in the law. How can we reconcile this? We must do it in the same way that Paul does. He says simply in Phi 3:9-10 that the blamelessness he had in the law was of his own doing, but that is not enough without the power of the resurrected Christ. It is only through the kind of blamelessness found in succumbing to Christ that we gain true righteousness.

What will we say then of Zechariah and Elizabeth? I would earnestly contend that they had been blamelessly obedient in anxious anticipation of the coming Christ, contrasted with Paul's blameless obedience in initial defiance of the risen Christ. Paul found his legal perfection to be insufficient, and as Gabriel states Zechariah found his legal perfection as fulfilled giving of a son who would walk not only in obedience, but in power and in Spirit.

ASV Luke 1:13 "But the angel said unto him, Fear not, Zacharias: because thy supplication is heard, and thy wife Elisabeth shall bear thee a son, and thou shalt call his name John."

ASV Luk 1:14 And thou shalt have joy and gladness; and many shall rejoice at his birth.

ASV Luk 1:15 For he shall be great in the sight of the Lord, and he shall drink no wine nor strong drink; and he shall be filled with the Holy Spirit, even from his mother's womb.

ASV Luk 1:16 And many of the children of Israel shall be turn unto the Lord their God.

ASV Luk 1:17 And he shall go before his face in the spirit and power of Elijah, to turn the hearts of the fathers to the children, and the disobedient *to walk* in the wisdom of the just; to make ready for the Lord a people prepared *for him*.

Zechariah and Elizabeth found themselves blessed by their blamelessness; urged and driven to move forward in the same direction, finding fulfillment in the natural progression of their faith. Their blameless obedience was in accordance with faith and the promises of God's kingdom. Paul, by contrast, found himself challenged by his blamelessness; confronted and changed by his discovery of true righteousness he changed directions and developed true faith. His blameless legalism was originally in direct opposition to the faith and promises of God's kingdom.

We see then, clearly, that blameless does in no way imply sinless. Rather, blameless implies compliance to the law in both these cases, and it is the condition of the person's righteousness and faith that determines their condition before God. Blameless compliance to the law is not enough; blameless in accordance with self reliant works is insufficient, while blameless in accordance with faith puts us in a right relationship with God.

Miracles of Jesus

Miracle	Matthew	Mark	Luke	John
Turned Water To Wine				John 2:1-11
Cast Demons Out In Capernaum		Mark 1:21-28	Luke 4:31-37	
Healed every disease	Matt 4:23-25	Mark 1:39		
Miraculous Catch of Fish			Luke 5:1-11	
Jesus' name casts out demons and heals many	Matt 7:22	Mark 9:38-40, 16:17	Luke 9:49-50, 10:17	John 1:12-13. 2:23, 3:18, 14:13-14, 17:11-12
Cured Leper	Matt 8:1-4	Mark 1:40-45	Luke 5:12-16	
Cured Centurion's Servant	Matt 8:5-13		Luke 7:1-10	
Cured Royal Official's Son				John 4:46-54
Cured Peter's Mother-in-law	Matt 8:14-17	Mark 1:29-34	Luke 4:38-41	
Drove 7 Demons out of Mary Magdalene		Mark 16:9	Luke 8:2	
Calmed The Sea	Matt 8:23-27	Mark 4:35-41	Luke 8:22-25	
Healed the Demoniac in the Tombs	Matt 8:28-34	Mark 5:1-20	Luke 8:26-39	
Cured a Paralytic at Capernaum	Matt 9:1-8	Mark 2:1-12	Luke 5:17-26	

Miracle	Matthew	Mark	Luke	John
Cured aPparalytic at the Pool of Bethesda				John 5:1-18
Raised the Son of a Widow at Nain			Luke 7:11-17	
Raised Jairus' Daughter	Matt 9:18-26	Mark 5:21-43	Luke 8:40-56	
Healed Woman with Hemorrhage	Matt 9:20-22	Mark 5:24-34	Luke 8:43-48	
Healed Two Blind Men, a Mute, and every disease and ailment	Matt 9:27-35			
Twelve Apostles given authority to cast out demons and raise the dead	Matt 10:1, 10:8	Mark 3:13-15, 6:7	Luke 9:1	
Unspecified miracles at Chorazin, Bethsaida, Capernaum	Matt 11:20-24		Luke 10:13-15	
Healed Man with Withered Hand	Matt 12:9-13	Mark 3:1-6	Luke 6:6-11	
Healed Many	Matt 12:15-21	Mark 3:7-12	Luke 6:17-19	
Healed a Blind-Mute Demoniac	Matt 12:22-32	Mark 3:20-30	Luke 11:14-23; 12:10	
Feeding of 5,000	Matt 14:13-21	Mark 6:30-44	Luke 9:10-17	John 6:1-14
Walked on Water	Matt 14:22-33	Mark 6:45-52		John 6:15-21

Miracle	Matthew	Mark	Luke	John
All those who touched Him / fringes of His garment were healed	Matt 14:34-36	Mark 6:53-56		
Cast Demon out of Canaanite / Syro-Phoenecian Woman	Matt 15:21-28	Mark 7:24-30		
Healed a Deaf-Mute		Mark 7:31-37		
Healed many crippled, blind and mute	Matt 15:29-31			
Feeding of 4,000	Matt 15:32-39	Mark 8:1-10		
Healed Blind Man at Bethsaida		Mark 8:22-26		
Cast Demon out of Boy	Matt 17:14-21	Mark 9:14-29	Luke 9:37-43	
Coin from Fish's Mouth	Matt 17:23-27			
Healed Woman on the Sabbath			Luke 13:10-17	
Continued to cast out demons			Luke 13:31-32	
Raised Lazarus from the Dead				John 11:1-44
Healed a Man with Dropsy			Luke 14:1-6	
Healed Ten Lepers			Luke 17:11-19	
Healed many in Judea	Matt 19:1-2			

Miracle	Matthew	Mark	Luke	John
Healed two Blind Men	Matt 20:29-34			
Healed Blind Beggar Bartimaeus		Mark 10:46-52	Luke 18:35-43	
Healed Blind Man				John 9
Healed Blind and Lame at Temple	Matt 21:14			
Cursed a fig tree	Matt 21:18-22	Mark 11:12-14, 11:20-25		
Healed High Priest's servant's, Malchus, Ear			Luke 22:49-51	
Many dead raised when Jesus died	Matt 27:50-54			
Empty Tomb / Jesus' Resurrection	Matt 27:62–28:15	Mark 16:1–8	Luke 24:1–12	John 20:1-10
Ascended to Heaven		Mark 16:19-20	Luke 24:50-53	John 20:17
2nd Miraculous Catch of Fish				John 21:1-14

Parables of Jesus

PARABLE	MATTHEW	MARK	LUKE
The Lamp	5:14-16	4:21-25	8:16-18
The Speck and The Log	7:1-5		6:37-42
New Cloth on Old Garment	9:16-17	2:21-22	5:36-39
The Divided Kingdom	12:24-30	3:23-27	11:14-23
The Sower	13:1-23	4:1-20	8:4-15
The Growing Seed		4:26-29	
The Good Samaritan			10:29-37
The Friend at Midnight			11:5-13
The Rich Fool			12:13-21
The Barren Fig Tree			13:6-9
The Weeds Among the Wheat	13:24-30		
The Mustard Seed	13:31-32	4:30-34	13:18-19
The Leaven	13:33-34		13:20-21
Hidden Treasure	13:44		
Pearl of Great Price	13:45-46		
The Net	13:47-50		
The Invited Guests			14:7-14
The Heart of Man	15:10-20	7:14-23	
The Lost Sheep	18:10-14		15:1-7
The Lost Coin			15:8-10
The Prodigal Son			15:11-32
The Rich Man & Lazarus			16:19-31
The Persistent Widow			18:1-8
The Pharisee and The Publican			18:9-14

The Unforgiving Servant	18:23-35		
Laborers in the Vineyard	20:1-16		
The Two Sons	21:28-32		
The Tenant Farmers	21:33-45	12:1-12	20:9-19
Marriage Feast or Great Banquet	22:1-14		14:15-24
The Budding Fig Tree	24:32-35	13:28-33	21:29-33
The Faithful vs. The Wicked Servant	24:45-51	13:34-37	12:35-48
The Ten Virgins	25:1-13		
Ten Talents or Gold Coins	25:14-30		19:11-27

Matthew, Fulfill the Old Law

The table on the following several pages is an essentially complete list of those citations, allusions, and formal quotes of the Old Testament and select extra-Biblical writings found in Matthew. In some cases, the specifics of the quotation are difficult to discern. Usually, these are due to translational differences between the Masoretic Text (MT) and the Septuagint (LXX). In these cases, it is the English re-rendering that falls short; the MT and LXX are in well-accepted formal or idiomatic agreement. Comparisons with the Mark or Luke accounts typically clarify the difficulties, and when those still bear difficulty comparisons within the Old Testament of parallel accounts provide the clarity.

Matthew	Old Testament Ref.	Citation / Allusion
1:1-17	Abraham / the seed of Abraham, through whom all nations would be blessed Gen.18:18; 22:15-18 Judah / ruling authority would not pass from Judah Gen.49:10 David / Jesus could legally be king / who would have an eternal kingdom Sam.7:2; Isa.11:1,2-6; 9:6 Jehoiachin (a.k.a. Jeconiah) / descendent of Joseph would not be able to sit on the throne of David / Christ's adoption into Joseph's line rather than descent from Joseph's line Jer.22:30 Zerubbabel / God says that the grandson of Jehoiachin would have ruling authority Hag.2:23 signet ring of authority that God promised he would deny Jehoiachin, Jer.22:24;	Jesus' genealogy verifies accounts in multiple OT sources, as well as allusions to many promises.

Matthew	Old Testament Ref.	Citation / Allusion
1:16	The title "Christ"	Title used by OT passages referring to the deliverer, the Messiah / understood to apply to a single individual / serves as a reference back to all recognized messianic OT texts
1:20	"Son of David"	David through adoption by Joseph / Davidic covenant anointed one from the line of David would sit on his throne to rule the world for all time. Jer.22:30; Sam.7:2; Isa.11:1,2-6; 9:6
1:21-23	Isa.7:14	Virgin birth Name 'Emmanuel' transliterated from Jesus (Joshua)
2:4	The title "Christ"	c.f. 1:16

Matthew	Old Testament Ref.	Citation / Allusion
2:6	Mic.5:2 2Sam.5:2 1Chr.11:2	Jesus to be born in Bethlehem. (a ruler born in Bethlehem, one whose days are of eternity, will arise from Judah to rule the earth.)
2:15	Hos.11:1	Flight to Egypt (Also alludes to type of Joshua entering Palestine & Judah returning from Babylonian exile.)
2:16,18	Jer.31:15	Killing newborns (Also alludes to type of Moses)
2:23	Judges 5-7; 16:17; Zech.3:8; 6:12; Isa.4:2	Jesus to be from Nazareth (lowly origins). Also, possibly, a play on words as the Hebrew for 'branch' is 'nezer'.
3:1-3	Isa.40:3	Quote

Matthew	Old Testament Ref.	Citation / Allusion
3:3-11	Isa.40:3-5	John the Baptizer, comes not only in the type of ministry of Elijah, but in his style. (See also Job 20:26 and Isa 34:8-10; 66:24. Elijah's style was very similar, see 2 Ki 1:8. Message was very similar see Hos 6:13)
3:9	Abraham	Illustration
3:12	Dan 12:1-3	Language chosen alludes to OT prophecies of God's Kingdom
3:15	Israel	Allusion
4:2	Gen.6-9 Ex.34:28 1Ki.19:8	40 days / nights Antitype of the flood judgment, Moses fasting before God on Sinai, and Elijah's fast to Horeb. All correspond to 40 years in the wilderness, and all precede God's deliverance

Matthew	Old Testament Ref.	Citation / Allusion
4:4 4:5-6 4:7 4:10	Deut. 8:3 Ps 91:11-12 Deut 6:13, 16	Many parallels with the wilderness wanderings.
4:13-16	Isa.9:1-7	Capernaum ministry Judgment will follow rebellion / Gentile connections
5:17	Law & Prophets	Fulfillment Promise
5:21	Ex.20:13 Deut.5:17	Formal Quote & Expansion on Meaning
5:27	Ex.20:14 Deut.5:18	Formal Quote & Expansion on Meaning
5:31	Deut.24:1	Formal Quote & Expansion on Meaning
5:38	Ex.21:24Lev.24:20	Formal Quote & Expansion on Meaning
5:43 (c.f. 19:19,22:39)	Lev.19:2,18	Formal Quote & Expansion on Meaning Application of Lev 19:2 refuting Rabbinical use of Lev 19:18

Matthew	Old Testament Ref.	Citation / Allusion
6:29	Solomon	Illustration
8:11	Abraham, Isaac & Jacob	Illustration / Allusion Ps.107:3; Isa.49:12; 59:19; Mal.1:11
8:17	Isa.53:4	Jesus Heals
8:20	Dan 7:13	Son of man 31x in Matthew; Jeremiah takes the title as a reference to humans. God repeatedly addresses Ezekiel as 'son of man.' Dan 7:13 identifies the 'Son of man' with the messiah.
9:6	Dan 7:13	Son of man c.f. 8:20
9:13	Hos.6:6	Formal Quote
9:18-26	1Ki.17 2Ki.4	Allusions to Elijah and Elisha The start of the ministries
9:27	Son of David	See 1:20
10:1	12 Disciples / 12 Tribes	Allusion Win the lost sheep of Israel.
10:15	Sodom & Gomorrah	Allusion Unbelieving Israel

Matthew	Old Testament Ref.	Citation / Allusion
10:18	Abrahamic Promise	Allusion God will redeem the Gentiles
10:23	Dan 7:13	Son of man c.f. 8:20
10:34-36	Micah 7:6	Possible allusion or possible borrowing of OT language style. See also Isa 10:3 and Hos 9:7; Israel's sin warrants judgment, the upright are no better than a 'mesuka' (thorny hedge), bringing their time of 'mebuka' (confusion). Micah's poetic version of 'the exalted are brought low'.
11:3	Isa.29:18; 35:5,6; Jer.6:21	Jesus is the Christ, the expected Messiah

Matthew	Old Testament Ref.	Citation / Allusion
11:10	Ex.23:20 Mal.3:1	Formal Quote Composite of Ex 23:20 and Mal 3:1 (Also found in Jewish literature, combines the LXX and MT)
11:14	Mal.3:1,23 (4:5-6)	John is the antitype of Elijah (c.f. 11:10; 17:13; Lk.1:17, 76f)
11:19	Dan 7:13	Son of man c.f. 8:20
11:21-22	Joel 3:4 Amos 1:9	Comparison with unbelieving Israel
11:23-24		Allusion to unbelieving Israel
11:28-30	Ecclus 51:23ff	Likely citation from the apocryphal book
12:3-4	Isa.21:6 Lev.24:5,9 Nu.28:9	David Christ heals on the Sabbath, David ate the consecrated bread on the Sabbath, but the priests condemn Christ's actions.
12:7	Hos.6:6	Formal Quote

Matthew	Old Testament Ref.	Citation / Allusion
12:8	Dan 7:13	Son of man is Lord of the harvest c.f. 8:20
12:17-21	Isa.42:1-4; 17-21 1Sam.42:1-4	Formal Quote Compares Christ's mission and Jonah's mission; both to those outside Israel as one of compassion. Analogy of a 3-day judgment.
12:23	Son of David	c.f. 1:20
12:32	Dan 7:13	Son of man c.f. 8:20
12:39-40	Jonah	Son of man c.f. 8:20
12:42	Queen of Sheba & Solomon	Intense curiosity of the Queen of Sheba contrasted with the indifference of the Pharisees, Sadducees and Scribes.

Matthew	Old Testament Ref.	Citation / Allusion
13:10-14	Isa.6:9-10 Deut.29:4 Jer.5:21 Ez.12:2	The wicked who wish not to submit to God will be granted their wish in the judgment.
13:14-15	Isa.6:9-10	Formal Quote Jesus' ministry will divide
13:31-35	Ezek.17:22-24	Formal Quote (v. 35)
13:32	Isa.4:2; 11:1; 14:19 Jer.23:5; 33:15 Zech.3:8	Illustration drawn from formal application during Isaiah's time. Possible historical analogy of progression.
13:35	Ps.78:2	Parabolic teaching See also Mark 4:33f
13:37,41	Dan 7:13	Son of man c.f. 8:20

Matthew	Old Testament Ref.	Citation / Allusion
15:4	Ex.20:12, 17 Deut.5:16	Formal Quote (For clarity from the Galilean Aramaic, see also Mark 7:10 and Luke 18:20. Compare those with the citations, and again in light of Ex 21:17. Again, consider Mark 7:6-7. Some quotes are difficult to discern in the English translations, being brought one from Hebrew, and another from Aramaic through Greek; consider parallel accounts as the best commentaries.)
15:8-9	Isa.29:13	Formal Quote c.f. 15:4
15:22	Son of David	c.f. 1:20

Matthew	Old Testament Ref.	Citation / Allusion
16:4	Jonah	3 days experience in the fish, used to predict the death, burial & resurrection of Christ
16:13	Dan 7:13	Son of man c.f. 8:20
16:14	Elijah, Jeremiah	Cited as possible identities of Christ by the disciples.
16:20	The title "Christ"	c.f. 1:16
16:27-28	Dan 7:13	Son of Man Mankind's punishment will fit his sin. (See also Ps 28:4; 62:12, Prov 24:12)
17:3-4	Moses; Elijah	Appeared at the transfiguration.
17:5	Ps.2:7 Isa.42:1 Deut. 18:15	Allusion to God's words at the transfiguration; language from the OT.
17:9	Dan.7:13	Son of man; resurrection c.f. 8:20

Matthew	Old Testament Ref.	Citation / Allusion
17:12	Mal.4:5-6	John is the antitype of Elijah; Son of man c.f. 11:14 and 8:20
17:22	Dan.7:13	Son of man c.f. 8:20
18:11	Dan.7:13	Son of man c.f. 8:20
18:16	Deut.19:15	Citation of the Old Law
19:4,5	Gen.2:24	Formal Quote (Again, for linguistic clarity, consider Mk 10:7 and Eph 5:31. The LXX helps understand the minor Hebrew confusion on this passage.)

Matthew	Old Testament Ref.	Citation / Allusion
19:18-19	Ex.20:12; Lev.19:18; Deut.5:16-20	Formal Quote (Again, for clarity, consider also: Mark 10:19 and Luke 18:20. Deut quote could be Lev 19:13 as the origination; also consider Deut 24:14 and Ex 21:10. Quote is most clear compared with the MT.)
19:28	Dan.7:13	Son of man c.f. 8:20
20:18	Dan.7:13	Son of man c.f. 8:20
20:28	Dan.7:13	Son of man c.f. 8:20
20:30-31	Son of David	Son of David c.f. 1:20
21:5	Isa.62:11 Zech.9:9	Formal Quote Triumphal Entry is on a young donkey (See also Jn 12:15)

Matthew	Old Testament Ref.	Citation / Allusion
21:9, 15	Ps.118:25f	Hosanna & Son of David (See also Mk 11:9f, Lk 19:37f) c.f. 1:20
21:13	Isa.56:7 Jer.7:11	Formal Quote (For clarity, consider also: Mk 11:17, Lk 19:46; first half matches the LXX, second half consistent with the MT.)
21:16	Ps.8:2	Formal Quote (Unique to Matthew)
21:42	Ps.118:22-23	Formal Quote Rejection of Christ by Jews
22:32	Ex.3:6	Formal Quote
22:37	Deut.6:4-5	Formal Quote
22:39	Lev.19:18	Formal Quote
22:41-45	David, Son of David, the title "Christ"	c.f. 1:20
22:43-44	Ps.110:1	Formal Quote Descendent of David Christ Glorified c.f. 1:20
23:2	Moses 'Seat'	Illustration
23:35	Abel, Zechariah	Illustration

Matthew	Old Testament Ref.	Citation / Allusion
23:39	Ps.118:26	Comparative Citation See also Luke 13:35
24:5	The title 'Christ'	c.f. 1:16
24:15	Dan.9:27; 12:11	Comparative Citation See also Mark 13:14
24:23	The title 'Christ'	c.f. 1:16
24:27	Dan.7:13	Son of man c.f. 8:20
24:30	Dan.7:13	Son of man c.f. 8:20
24:37-38	Dan.7:13	Noah; son of man
24:39	Dan.7:13	Son of man c.f. 8:20
24:44	Dan.7:13	Son of man c.f. 8:20
25:31	Dan.7:13	Son of man c.f. 8:20
26:2	Dan.7:13	Son of man c.f. 8:20
26:24	Dan.7:13	Son of man c.f. 8:20
26:31	Zech.13:7	Formal Quote Cowardice of disciples
26:45	Dan.7:13	Son of man c.f. 8:20

Matthew	Old Testament Ref.	Citation / Allusion
26:54-56	Zech.13:7	Allusion to Jesus arrest
26:63,68	The title 'Christ'	c.f. 1:16
26:64	Dan 7:13	Son of man c.f. 8:20
27:9-10	Zech.11:12-13	Formal Quote Judas' death. Matthew attributes the quote to Jeremiah, demonstrating that he is simultaneously alluding to Jer 19, the potter's field, and citing Zech 11.
27:35	Ps.22:18	Allusion
27:46	Ps.22:1	Allusion
27:15, 57	Isa.53:9	Fulfillment. Joseph is a rich man by Matthew's account (note that Mark 15:43 simply cites him as respected councilman, but that is consistent).

Complete Harmony Table

For this Table I have divided Jesus' life into the same 14 segments used for the Simplified Harmony Table. The bold 'summaries' breaking out each section include the simplified scripture references for that portion of the Harmony. You will note that some of the specific verses vary slightly from those summaries. The detailed Harmony takes into account single and pairs of verses that fit into the general scheme of the overall section. In contrast, the 10 summary statements are intended only to group larger sections of scripture.

	Matthew	Mark	Luke	John
Jesus Before Time Began. He is Everywhere and Everywhen, Lasting Forever. (John 1:1-3)				
Jesus Before Time Began				1:1-18
Jesus' Birth and Childhood. Circa 5 BC, lasting approximately 30 years, taking place in Bethlehem, Egypt, and Galilee. (Matt 1-2, Luke 1-2)				
Jesus' Lineage through Joseph	1:1-17			
Jesus' Lineage, Apparently through Mary			3:23-38	

	Matthew	Mark	Luke	John
John the Baptizer Foretold			1:1-25	
Gabriel visits Mary			1:26-38	
Mary visits Elizabeth in Judea			1:39-56	
John the Baptizer Born			1:57-80	
Angel Tells Joseph To Wed Mary	1:18-25			
Birth of Jesus in Bethlehem			2:1-7	
Shepherds visit Jesus			2:8-20	
Circumcision of Jesus			2:21	
Jesus presented in the Temple			2:22-38	
Magi From the East Visit Jesus	2:1-12			
Joseph, Mary and Jesus Flee to Egypt	2:13-15			
Herod Executes Baby Boys	2:16-18			
Joseph, Mary and Jesus Return To Nazareth	2:19-23		2:39	

	Matthew	Mark	Luke	John
Jesus Left in Jerusalem (At Temple)			2:40-52	

John The Baptizer. Circa 25 AD, lasting about 2 years, taking place throughout Cana, Judea, and near the Jordan. (Matt 3:1-12, Mark 1:1-18, Luke 3:1-20)

	Matthew	Mark	Luke	John
John the Baptizer	3:1-12	1:1-8	3:1-20	

Jesus' Baptism. Circa 27 AD, in the Jordan River south of Nazareth. (Matt 3:13-17, Mark 1:9-11, Luke 3:21-22)

	Matthew	Mark	Luke	John
John the Baptizer Baptizes Jesus	3:13-17	1:9-11	3:21-23	

Jesus Fasts & Is Tempted. Circa 27 AD, lasting 40 days, in the Wilderness near Galilee. (Matt 4:1-11, Mark 1:12-13, Luke 4:1-13)

	Matthew	Mark	Luke	John
Jesus Fasts 40 Days / Tempted in the Wilderness	4:1-11	1:12-13	4:1-13	
John's Witness of the Christ				1:19-28
John's Treatise on Jesus' Baptism				1:29-34
The 1st Disciples				1:35-51

	Matthew	Mark	Luke	John

Jesus' Pre-Ministry Miracle. Circa 27 AD, at a Wedding Feast lasting 1 week, in Cana of Galilee. (John 2:1-12)

	Matthew	Mark	Luke	John
Jesus' 1st Miracle: Water to Wine				2:1-12

Jesus' Early Judean Ministry. Circa 27 AD, lasting about 2 months, primarily in Judea. (John 2:13-4:3)

	Matthew	Mark	Luke	John
1st Cleansing of the Temple				2:13-25
Jesus Tells Nicodemus of Being Reborn				3:1-21
Many Baptized in Judea				3:22-24
John's Final Testimony of Jesus the Christ				3:25-36
Herod imprisons John the Baptist	4:12	1:14	(3:19-20)	

Jesus' Visit to Samaria. Circa 27 AD, for about 1 month, traveling north from Judea toward Cana in Galilee, passing through Sychar and Samaria. (John 4:4-42)

	Matthew	Mark	Luke	John
Jesus withdraws from Judea				4:1-3
Jesus and the Samaritan Woman at the Well				4:4-26

	Matthew	Mark	Luke	John
Disciples question Jesus				4:27-38
Samaritans come to Jesus				4:39-42
Jesus continues toward Galilee			4:14-15	4:43
Jesus' 1st Rejection in Nazareth			4:16-30	
Arrival in Cana of Galilee				4:43-45
Jesus Heals the Royal Official's Son				4:46-54

Jesus' Galilean Ministry. Begins likely in late 27 AD, lasting approximately 2 years, remaining primarily in Galilee. (Matt 4:12-19:1, Mark 1:14-10:1, Luke 4:14-9:62, John 4:43-54 & John 6)

	Matthew	Mark	Luke	John
Jesus Remains in Capernaum	4:13-17	1:14-15	4:31-32	
Disciples to be Fishers of Men	4:18-22	1:16-20		
Jesus Casts Demon out at Capernaum Synagogue		1:21-28	4:33-37	
Jesus Heals Peter's Mother-In-Law	8:14-17	1:29-31	4:38-39	
Jesus Heals Many		1:32-34	4:40-41	

	Matthew	Mark	Luke	John
Disciples Come to Jesus		1:35-38	4:42-43	
Jesus preaches in the Synagogues	4:23-25	1:39	4:44	
Jesus preaches from Simon's boat			5:1-3	
Miraculous Catch of Fish			5:4-11	
Jesus Heals a Leper	8:2-4	1:40-45	5:12-16	
Jesus Cures Paralytic, Lowered Through Roof	9:2-8	2:1-12	5:17-26	
Matthew (Levi) Called to Discipleship	9:9	2:13-14	5:27-28	
Jesus' Discourse: New Wineskin, New Cloth	9:10-17	2:15-22	5:29-39	

Jesus' Visit to Jerusalem. Possibly spring 28 AD, certainly during the Galilean Ministry, lasting about 1 month in Jerusalem, then returning to minister in Galilee.
(John 5)

	Matthew	Mark	Luke	John
Jesus: Passover in Jerusalem				5:1
Jesus Heals Paralytic at Pool of Bethesda				5:2-15
Jesus Answers for Healing on the Sabbath				5:16-47

	Matthew	Mark	Luke	John
Return to Galilean Ministry...				
Disciples Pick Grain on the Sabbath	12:1-8	2:23-28	6:1-5	
Jesus Heals Man's Hand on the Sabbath	12:9-14	3:1-6	6:6-11	
Jesus Withdraws to the Sea of Galilee	12:14-21	3:7		
Great Crowds Pressed Jesus for Healing	4:23-25	3:7-12		
Jesus Prays			6:12	
Jesus Names the 12 Apostles	(10:2-4)	3:13-19	6:13-16	
Jesus Heals Many			6:17-19	
Jesus Goes to the Hilltop	5:1			
"Sermon on the Mount"	5:1-8:1		6:20-49	
The Centurion of Great Faith: Jesus Heals His Servant	8:5-13		7:1-10	
Jesus Raises Widow's Only Son from Dead at Nain			7:11-17	
John Asks Jesus for Confirmation & Comfort	11:2-6		7:18-23	

	Matthew	Mark	Luke	John
Jesus Assures John the Baptizer	11:7-19		7:24-35	
Woe To Unrepentant Cities	11:20-30			
Jesus Eats With Simon the Pharisee			7:36-50	
Jesus Travels City to City with Supportive Women			8:1-3	
Jesus Heals Blind-Mute Demoniac	12:22-23	3:20-22		
Jesus Rebukes Pharisees	12:24-37	3:22-30		
Jesus Discourse: The Sign of Jonah	12:38-45			
Jesus Family Tries to Take Him Home	12:46-50	3:31-35	8:19-21	
Parables: Sower, Explained, Tares, Mustard Seed, Leaven	13:1-35	4:1-34	8:4-18	
Parables: Tares Explained, Hidden Treasure, Pearl of Great Price, Dragnet	13:36-53			
Jesus & Disciples Cross Sea of Galilee	8:18	4:35	8:22	
Jesus Calms the Sea	8:23-27	4:36-41	8:23-25	

	Matthew	Mark	Luke	John
Jesus Casts Demon Out (Legion)	8:28-34	5:1-20	8:26-39	
Jesus Crosses Over to Capernaum	9:1	5:21	8:40	
Jairus Asks Jesus to Heal his Daughter	9:18-19	5:22-23	8:41-42	
Woman with Hemorrhage Touches Jesus and is Healed	9:20-22	5:24-34	8:42-48	
Jairus' Daughter Dies		5:35-36	8:49-50	
Jesus Raises Jairus' Daughter from the Dead	9:23-26	5:37-43	8:51-56	
Jesus Heals Two Blind Men	9:27-31			
Jesus Heals Mute Demoniac	9:32-34			
Jesus Again Rejected in Nazareth	13:54-58	6:1-6		
The 12 Sent Out	9:35-11:1	6:7-13	9:1-6	
John the Baptizer Dies	14:1-12			
Herod Believes Jesus to be John the Baptizer Risen		6:14-29	9:7-9	

	Matthew	Mark	Luke	John
The 12 Return, Then Withdraw	14:13	6:30-32	9:10	6:1
Jesus Teaches, Heals Many	14:14	6:33-34	9:11	6:2
Jesus Feeds the 5,000	14:15-21	6:35-44	9:12-17	6:3-14
Jesus Sends the Disciples Ahead and Prays Alone	14:22-23	6:45-47		6:15
Jesus Walks on the Water	14:24-27	6:48-52		6:16-21
Peter Walks on the Water	14:28-33			
Jesus Heals all who Touch Him at Gennesaret	14:34-36	6:53-56		
"I Am the Bread of Life"				6:22-7:1
Jesus Rebukes Human Tradition	15:1-11	7:1-16		
Jesus Discourse on Speech and the Heart	15:12-20	7:17-23		
Jesus Heals Syrophoenician Woman's Daughter	15:21-28	7:24-30		
Jesus Heals Deaf Man		7:31-37		
Jesus Heals Many	15:29-31			

	Matthew	Mark	Luke	John
Jesus Feeds the 4,000	15:32-39	8:1-10		
Pharisees Seek a Sign from Jesus	16:1-4	8:11-13		
Jesus' Discourse on Leaven of Pharisees	16:5-12	8:13-21		
Jesus Heals Blind man at Pool of Bethsaida		8:22-26		
Peter's Great Confession of Jesus as Christ	16:13-20	8:27-30		
Jesus Rebukes Peter & Predicts His Death	16:21-28	8:31-9:1	9:18-27	
Jesus is Transfigured	17:1-8	9:2-8	9:28-36	
The Sign of Elijah Precedes the Christ	17:9-13	9:9-13		
Jesus Casts Demon out of Boy	17:14-18	9:14-27	9:37-43	
Jesus' Discourse on Faith as a Mustard Seed	17:19-21	9:28-29		
Jesus Foretells His Death	17:22-23	9:30-32	9:44-45	
Jesus Pays Tax with Coin From Fish's Mouth	17:24-27			
Apostles Claim Greatness in the Kingdom	18:1-6	9:33-37	9:46-48	

	Matthew	Mark	Luke	John
John Tries to Stop Others from Casting Demons Out		9:38-42	9:49-50	
Jesus Warns About Stumbling Blocks (Pluck Eye)	18:7-11	9:43-50		
Brief Parable of The Lost Sheep	*18:12-14*			
Jesus' Discourse on Discipline and Prayer	18:15-20			
Peter's Question About Forgiveness (70 times 7), Parable of Unforgiving Servant	*18:21-35*			

Jesus' Later Judean Ministry. Likely mid or late 29 AD, lasting about 1 month, throughout Judea including Perea and Bethany.
(Luke 10:1-13:21, John 7:1-10:39)

	Matthew	Mark	Luke	John
Feast of Booths				7:2
Jesus' Brothers Urge Him to Go to Judea				7:3-8
Jesus Remains in Galilee				7:9
Jesus Sets out for Jerusalem			9:51	7:10
Messengers Sent Ahead to Samaria			9:52-53	

	Matthew	Mark	Luke	John
James and John Want to Call Fire From Heaven			9:54-56	
False Discipleship	8:19-22		9:57-62	
People Fear those Opposed to Jesus				7:11-13
Jesus at the Temple				7:14-15
Jesus Foretells Those Who Seek His Death				7:16-19
Jesus Defends Healing on the Sabbath				7:20-24
Jesus Reaffirms that He is From God				7:25-30
Many Signs and Wonders				7:31
Pharisees Try to Capture Jesus				7:32-36
Last day of Feast of Booths				7:37
Jesus' Discourse on Living Water				7:37-39
Division among the Disciples / People				7:40-44
Pharisees Seek Evidence Against Jesus				7:45-47

	Matthew	Mark	Luke	John
Judgement of Nicodemus				7:48-53
Jesus goes to the Mount of Olives				8:1
Teaches at temple in the morning				8:2
Adulterous woman brought to Jesus				8:3-11
"I Am The Light"				8:12-20
Sent by the Father				8:21-30
Jesus' Teaching at the Temple				8:31-59
Jesus heals a man born blind				9:1-7
Neighbors question the former blind man				9:8-12
Pharisees question man's parents				9:13-34
Jesus finds the man				9:35-39
Pharisees ask if they are blind				9:40-10:6
"I Am The Good Shepherd"				10:7-18

	Matthew	Mark	Luke	John
Division among the Jews				10:19-21
Seventy sent out			10:1-16	
Seventy return			10:17-20	
Jesus Praises God for the Disciples			10:21-24	
Who is my neighbor?			10:25-28	
Parable of the Good Samaritan			*10:29-37*	
Jesus with Mary and Martha			10:38-42	
Jesus teaches the disciples how to pray			11:1-13	
Casts out Demon, House Divided			11:14-26	
Blessed Mary, Blessed Message			11:27-28	
Sign of Jonah			11:29-32	
The light is in you, light of the world			11:33-36	
Cleanse the Inside, Hypocrisy			11:37-44	

	Matthew	Mark	Luke	John
Jesus pronounces woes on the Lawyers			11:45-52	
Jesus leaves, and they plot against him.			11:53-54	
Jesus teaches a great crowd	==	==	12:1-12	==
Jesus warns against greed			12:13-15	
Parables about being ready			12:16-40	
Peter's question			12:41	
More parables			12:42-59	
Fate of Galileans reported to Jesus			13:1-5	
Parable of the fig tree			13:6-9	
Woman healed on the Sabbath			13:10-13	
Synagogue official opposes Jesus			13:14-17	
Parables of mustard seed and leaven			13:18-21	
Feast of Dedication in the temple				10:22-23

	Matthew	Mark	Luke	John
Jews confront Christ				10:24-39
Jesus goes to Aenon near Salim				10:40-42
Jesus travels toward Jerusalem			13:22	
How many will be saved?			13:23-30	
Pharisees warn Jesus about Herod			13:31-35	
In a Pharisee's house on the Sabbath			14:1	
Man with dropsy healed			14:2-6	
Parable of the guests			14:7-11	
Parable to the host of the feast			14:12-14	
Parable of the dinner			14:15-24	
Great multitudes travel with Jesus			14:25	
The cost of discipleship			14:25-35	
Eats with tax collectors and sinners			15:1-2	

	Matthew	Mark	Luke	John
Lost sheep, coin, and son			15:3-32	
Parable of the unrighteous steward			16:1-13	
Pharisees scoff. Teaching on divorce.			16:14-18	
The rich man and Lazarus			16:19-31	
Jesus instructs disciples			17:1-10	
Lazarus of Bethany reported sick				11:1-6
Jesus delays for 2 days				11:6
Jesus prepares 12 to go to Judea				11:7-16
Arrives near Bethany, 2 days later				11:17-18
Martha meets Jesus				11:19-29
Mary comes to Jesus				11:30-37
Jesus comes to the tomb				11:38
Jesus raises Lazarus from the dead				11:39-44

	Matthew	Mark	Luke	John
Unbelievers report to Pharisees				11:45-46
Conspiracy to kill Jesus				11:47-53
Jesus goes to Ephraim				11:54
Ten lepers are cleansed			17:11-14	
Samaritan returns to thank Jesus			17:15-19	
Pharisees ask about the Kingdom			17:20-21	
Jesus warns disciples about the future			17:22-37	
Parable of the unjust judge			18:1-8	
Parable of the Pharisee and tax collector			18:9-14	
Jesus goes to Judea by the Jordan	19:1	10:1		
Multitudes follow Jesus	19:2			
Pharisees question Jesus about divorce	19:3-9	10:2-9		
Disciples question Jesus about divorce	19:10-12	10:10-12		

	Matthew	Mark	Luke	John
Jesus blesses little children	19:13-15	10:13-16	18:15-17	
Rich young ruler	19:16-26	10:17-27	18:18-27	
Disciples reward	19:27-30	10:28-31	18:28-30	
First shall be last discourse	20:1-16			
Jesus predicts death on road to Jerusalem	20:17-19	10:32-34	18:31-34	
Request for James and John	20:20-24	10:35-41		
Relationship of disciples to each other	20:25-28	10:42-45		
Blind men healed near Jericho	20:29-34	10:46-52	18:35-43	
Zaccheus is converted near Jericho			19:1-10	
Jesus is near Jerusalem			19:11	
Blind men healed near Jericho			19:12-27	
Journey toward Jerusalem for Passover				11:54
Jesus discussed by Jews and Priests				11:55-57

	Matthew	Mark	Luke	John
Jesus in Bethany				12:1
Mary anoints Jesus in Simon's house				12:2-8
Mary's deed recounted	26:6-13	14:3-9		
Crowds come to see Jesus and Lazarus				12:9
Chief priests conspire to kill Lazarus				12:10-11
Jesus ascends toward Jerusalem	21:1	11:1	19:28	
Two disciples get a colt	21:1-7	11:1-7	19:29-35	
Triumphal entry into Jerusalem	21:8-11	11:7-10	19:35-38	12:12-18
Pharisees reaction			19:39-40	12:19
Jesus weeps for Jerusalem			19:41-44	
Jesus enters Jerusalem then goes to Bethany		11:11		
Jesus curses a fig tree		11:12-14		
The 2nd temple cleansing	21:12-13	11:15-17	19:45-46	

	Matthew	Mark	Luke	John
Jesus heals many in the temple	21:14			
Jewish leaders seek to destroy Jesus	21:15-16	11:18	19:47-48	
Jesus leaves Jerusalem	21:17	11:19		
The withered fig tree (next morning)	21:18-22	11:20-26		
Authority challenged in the Temple	21:23-27	11:27-33	20:1-8	
Parable of the two sons	21:28-32			
Parable of the vine growers	21:33-46	12:1-12	20:9-18	
Parable of the wedding feast	22:1-14			
Jews question on paying taxes	22:15-22	12:13-17	20:19-26	
Sadducees question the resurrection	22:23-33	12:18-27	20:27-40	
Scribes and Pharisees question Jesus	22:34-40	12:28-34		
Jesus questions them about baptism	22:41-46	12:35-37	20:41-44	
Warnings about Scribes and Pharisees	23:1-39	12:38-40	20:45-47	

	Matthew	Mark	Luke	John
The widow's mite		12:41-44	21:1-4	
Disciples admire the temple	24:1-2	13:1-2	21:5-6	
4 fishermen question Jesus	24:3	13:3-4	21:7	
Jesus warns disciples of persecution	24:4-14	13:5-13	21:8-19	
Jesus predicts the fall of Jerusalem	24:15-28	13:14-23	21:20-24	
Jesus teaches about the 2nd coming	24:29-31	13:24-27	21:25-28	
Parable of the fig tree	24:32-33	13:28-29	21:29-31	
Warnings to be alert	24:34-51	13:30-37	21:32-36	
Parable of the 10 virgins	25:1-13			
Parable of the talents	25:14-30			
Warnings about the Judgment	25:31-46			
Jesus predicts day of crucifixion	26:1-2			
People come early to hear Jesus teach			21:37-38	

	Matthew	Mark	Luke	John
Greeks seek Jesus				12:20-22
Final public appeals to unbelievers				12:23-50
Plot to kill Jesus	26:3-5	14:1-2	22:1-2	
Judas bargains to betray Jesus	26:14-16	14:10-11	22:3-6	
Peter & John sent to prepare for Passover	26:17-19	14:12-16	22:7-13	
Fellowship in the upper room	26:20	14:17	22:14	
Jesus washes the disciples' feet				13:1-20
The Lord's Supper	26:26-29	14:22-25	22:14-20	I Cor 11:23-29
Jesus predicts his betrayal	26:21-25	14:18-21	22:21-23	13:21-26
Judas leaves				13:27-30
A new commandment				13:31-35
Dispute about the greatest disciple			22:24-30	
Jesus predicts the disciples' denial	26:31-32	14:27-28		

	Matthew	Mark	Luke	John
Jesus tells Simon he prayed for him			22:31-32	
Jesus predicts Peter's denials	26:33-35	14:29-31	22:33-34	13:36-38
Jesus warns the disciples to be prepared			22:35-38	
Jesus comforts the disciples				14:1-4
Jesus responds to Thomas				14:5-7
Jesus responds to Philip				14:8-21
Jesus responds to Judas not Iscariot				14:22-31
They sing a hymn and leave	26:30	14:26		14:31
The farewell discourse				15:1-16:33
Jesus prays for his disciples				17:1-26
The fellowship enters Gethsemane	26:36	14:32	22:39-40	18:1
Jesus prays in the Garden of Gethsemane	26:36-46	14:32-42	22:40-46	
Mob comes to arrest Jesus	26:47	14;43		18:2-3

	Matthew	Mark	Luke	John
Judas betrays Jesus with a kiss	26:48-50	14:44-45	22:47-48	
Jesus answers the mob with authority				18:4-9
Peter severs the ear of Malchus	26:50-54	14:46-47	22:49-50	18:10-11
Jesus heals the high priest's servant			22:51	
Jesus is arrested. The disciples flee.	26:55-56	14:48-52	22:52-54	18:12
Jesus lead to high priest's house	26:57	14:53	22:54	18:13-14
Peter follows at a distance	26:58	14:54	22:54	18:15-16
Peter's 1st denial - doorkeeping girl	26:69-70	14:66-68	22:55-57	18:17-18
Annas questions Jesus				18:19-24
Peter's 2nd denial - by the fire	26:71-72	14:69-70	22:58	18:25
Peter's 3rd denial - relative of Malchus	26:73-75	14:70-72	22:59-62	18:26-27
Guards beat Jesus			22:63-65	
False witnesses testify	26:59-61	14:55-59		

	Matthew	Mark	Luke	John
Caiaphas condemns Jesus	26:62-66	14:60-64	22:66-71	
Sanhedrin beats Jesus	26:67-68	14:65		
Jesus lead from Caiaphas to Praetorium				18:28
Remorse of Judas	27:1-10		Acts 1:16-20	
Jesus before Pilate	27:1-14		23:1-7	18:29-38
Jesus before Herod			23:8-10	
Herod's soldiers mock Jesus		15:1-5	23:11-12	
Pilate releases Barabbas	27:15-26	15:6-15	23:13-25	18:38-40
Pilate's soldiers crown and mock Jesus	27:27-30	15:16-20		19:1-3
Pilate tries to release Jesus				19:4-7
Pilate questions Jesus again				19:8-11
Pilate tries to release Jesus again				19:12
Pilate sentences Jesus				19:13-15

	Matthew	Mark	Luke	John
Pilate delivers Jesus to be crucified				19:16
Jesus carries the cross				19:17
Simon of Cyrene bears the cross	27:31-32	15:20-21	23:26	
Jesus speaks to weeping women			23:27-32	
Jesus is brought to Golgotha	27:33	15:22	23:32-33	19:17
Soldiers offer Jesus sour wine mix	27:34	15:23		
He is crucified on the 3rd hour		15:25		
2 robbers are crucified with Jesus	27:38	15:27-28	23:33	19:18
Inscription written by Pilate	27:37	15:26	23:38	19:19-22
"Forgive them…"			23:34	
Soldiers divide the garments of Jesus	27:35-36	15:24	23:34	19:23-24
"Behold your mother."				19:25-27
Multitudes mock Jesus	27:39-43	15:29-32	23:35-37	

	Matthew	Mark	Luke	John
Robbers mock Jesus	27:44	15:32	23:39	
One robber rebukes the other			23:40-41	
"…you will be with me in Paradise."			23:43	
Darkness from 6th to 9th hour	27:45	15:33	23:44-45	
"Eloi, Eloi, Lamma, Sabachthani"	27:46	15:34		
"I thirst."				19:28
Jesus is offered sour wine on a reed.	27:47-49	15:35-36		19:29-30
"It is finished."				19:30
Jesus cries out	27:50	15:37	23:46	
"Into Thy hands I commit my spirit."			23:46	
Jesus bows his head and dies	27:50	15:37	23:46	19:30
Temple veil torn from top to bottom	27:51	15:38	23:45	
Earthquake	27:51			

	Matthew	Mark	Luke	John
Saints rise after Christ's resurrection	27:52-53			
Centurion: "This was the Son of God"	27:54	15:39	23:47	
Multitude leaves grieving			23:48	
Women watch from a distance	27:55-56	15:40-41	23:49	
Request that legs be broken				19:31-32
Soldier pierces Jesus' side				19:33-34
Fulfilment of prophecy				19:35-37
Joseph requests body from Pilate	27:57-58	15:42-43	23:50-52	19:38
Centurion reports that Jesus is dead		15:44-45		
Joseph takes the body		15:45		19:38
Nicodemus and Joseph prepare the body				19:39-40
Body placed in new garden tomb	27:59-60	15:46	23:53	19:41-42
Two Marys watch the burial	27:61	15:47	23:54-55	

	Matthew	Mark	Luke	John
Roman soldiers guard the tomb	27:62-66			
Two Marys prepare burial spiced ointment			23:56	
Angel rolls stone	28:2-4			
Women bring spices to tomb at dawn	28:1	16:1-4	24:1-3	20:1
Angels appear to women	28:5-7	16:5-7	24:4-8	
Women run to tell disciples	28:8	16:8	24:9-11	20:2
Peter and John inspect the empty tomb			24:12	20:3-9
Peter and John go home			24:12	20:10
Mary Magdalene stands weeping				20:11
Mary sees two angels				20:12-13
Jesus appears to Mary Magdalene		16:9		20:14-17
Jesus appears to other women	28:9-10			
Women report to the disciples		16:10-11		20:18

	Matthew	Mark	Luke	John
Guards report to the priests	28:11-15			
Jesus meets 2 on road to Emmaus		16:12-13	24:13-32	
Jesus appears to Simon Peter	1st Cor 15:5		24:34	
Two report to disciples in Jerusalem			24:33-35	
Jesus appears to disciples without Thomas			24:36-46	20:19-24
Disciples report to Thomas				20:25
Jesus appears to disciples and Thomas		16:14		20:26-29
Jesus appears to seven by the sea				21:1-14
Jesus questions Peter 3 times				21:15-23
Jesus appears to 500 at one time	1st Cor 15:6			
Jesus appears to James	1st Cor 15:7			
Jesus commissions the apostles	28:16-20	16:15-18	24:44-49	
Jesus is received into Heaven		16:19-20	24:50-53	

	Matthew	Mark	Luke	John
John's first testimony				20:30-31
John's second testimony				21:24-25
Luke summarizes the 40 day appearances			Acts 1:4-11	
The Holy Spirit Indwells the Apostles			Acts 2:1-4	
Jesus Appears to Paul	1st Cor 15:8		Acts 9:3	

Blank Pages

Last Page Marker